The media's watching
Here's a sampling of o

VAULT GUIDE TO
TECHNOLOGY CAREERS

VAULT GUIDE TO
TECHNOLOGY
CAREERS

**TOD EMKO, EVAN KOBLENTZ
AND THE STAFF OF VAULT**

For information about permission to reproduce selections from this book, contact Vault Inc., 150 W. 22nd St., 5th Floor, New York, NY 10011, (212) 366-4212.

Library of Congress CIP Data is available.

ISBN 1-58131-289-X

Printed in the United States of America

ACKNOWLEDGMENTS

From Tod Emko:

This book couldn't have been made without the help of Caroline Harzewski, John Challenger of Challenger, Gray & Christmas, Tracey Losco of New York University, and numerous other friends in technology who lent their guidance. Having a small army of ears to the ground is invaluable and often necessary when reporting on this ever-changing field. My co-workers at ToastedPixel.com also did a great job of helping out and holding down the fort while my attentions were on this book. Special thanks to John Running, Clay Givens, and Greg Land, who went above and beyond the call in continually giving their knowledge and insights.

From Evan Koblentz:

Thanks to Mom and Dad, for teaching me about hard work, and to Tom, for the brain download.

From Vault:

We are extremely grateful to Vault's entire staff for all their help in the editorial, production and marketing processes. Vault also would like to acknowledge the support of our investors, clients, employees, family, and friends. Thank you!

Table of Contents

Visit Vault at **www.vault.com** for insider company profiles, expert advice,
career message boards, expert resume reviews, the Vault Job Board and more.

VAULT CAREER LIBRARY   ix

Chapter 5: The IT Interview   65

ON THE JOB   75

Chapter 6: Career Paths and Days in the Life 77

Chapter 7: Lifestyle in Tech   95

APPENDIX   99

Introduction

Information technology is the professional field that creates and maintains the computers and related systems that keep modern society interconnected and comfortable. Commonly known as IT, for information technology, tech affects all aspects of modern life, from ordinary e-mail to maintaining nuclear defense systems. Contrary to the stereotype, the industry isn't just for pasty-skinned nerds, but has room for a wide range of personality types. Historically, salaries have been generous, and in the past decade, the possibility of making a mint in stock options has emerged as an especially delicious bonus.

But technology is no longer an easy ride to, if not fame and fortune, at least a very comfortable career. The technology market in the United States has suffered in the past three years, losing approximately 400,000 jobs between 2001 and April 2004, according to a report sponsored by the Ford Foundation. Some formerly hot markets, like San Francisco and Boston, have suffered disproportionately. And the evaporation of the dot-com craze has meant fewer golden stock options on offer.

On the other hand, few other careers offer what technology careers can – meritocracy, high salaries, teamwork and intellectual fulfillment. For logicians, machinery-lovers and people-people alike, technology careers continue to be attractive. And while the field may suffer fluctuations, those willing to refresh their skill set find themselves continually employable.

Use the Internet's
MOST TARGETED
job search tools.

Vault Job Board

Target your search by industry, function, and experience level, and find the job openings that you want.

VaultMatch Resume Database

Vault takes match-making to the next level: post your resume and customize your search by industry, function, experience and more. We'll match job listings with your interests and criteria and e-mail them directly to your inbox.

V∧ULT

> the most trusted name in career information™

THE SCOOP

IT Basics and Trends

CHAPTER 1

What's in a Computer?

Whether sketching out plans for brand-new software programs at a major technology firm like IBM or backing up files at a small insulation materials company, technology professionals work with computers, computer software and computer systems.

The cartography of a modern IT environment can be very complex. Here's a simplified view of the five major parts: desktops, servers, networks, storage, and software.

Desktop computers

Desktop computers are the simplest part, using commodity components that are more easily replaced than fixed. Add a keyboard, monitor, mouse, and network connection, and it's ready to use. Most corporate desktops today run the Windows 2000 or Windows XP operating systems. They typically run office suite software, which includes programs for word processing, e-mail, spreadsheets, and presentations, such as Microsoft Office, Sun Microsystems' StarOffice, or the open-source OpenOffice package. Users with intensive graphical or engineering requirements may use Apple Macintosh computers, or workstation computers from Silicon Graphics or Sun Microsystems.

Servers

Servers are more complicated. The basic idea is the same as any desktop computer, but the reliability and the purpose differ greatly. Servers typically use physically stronger components; they have redundancy in the network connections, power supplies, and cooling fans; and they use more stable operating systems such as Windows Server or various versions of Unix (including Linux). Like a pickup truck vs. a passenger car, they also do away with consumer features, such as disk drives, speakers, and fancy colors. Whereas desktop computers are abandoning the traditional beige box shape, in favor of colors and shapes that are more decorative, server computers also now come in different models, but for purposes of maintenance and density. Examples include rack-mounted servers and so-called "pizza box" designs, server blades, and clusters for high availability. Servers also run special

Visit Vault at **www.vault.com** for insider company profiles, expert advice, career message boards, expert resume reviews, the Vault Job Board and more.

VAULT CAREER LIBRARY   5

software for system monitoring – since they cost much more than desktops, it's important to perform preventative maintenance. The largest organizations also may have mainframes or supercomputers, which put simply, are ultra-large and ultra-fast servers, respectively.

Networks

Networks are the infrastructure that connects all the other parts for the purpose of sharing data. Networks include management software (such as BMC Software's Patrol, Cisco's CiscoWorks, Computer Associates' Unicenter, Hewlett Packard's OpenView, IBM's Tivoli, and several others), wires (such as Ethernet, Gigabit Ethernet, and Fibre Channel), special ports to plug in the wires (NICs – "network interface cards" – please don't call it a "NIC card"), and bridges, routers, and switches (the appliance-like boxes that serve as interchanges on the data highway). Networks also may use special appliances for monitoring, remote and wireless access, security, and testing.

Storage

Storage generally refers to the refrigerator-sized boxes, stuffed with hard drives and a management system, where large enterprises keep all their data. As described in the trends section of this book, most storage today is either in a SAN (storage area network) or NAS (network attached storage) configuration. There are still many stand-alone storage units in the field, but the companies that make enterprise storage discourage it (such as EMC Corp., Hewlett-Packard, IBM, Network Appliance, and Sun Microsystems). Storage is attached to backup systems, which include software and magnetic tape libraries. As data ages, it gets moved from the expensive storage to the tapes, and newer data is put onto the expensive storage, in a never-ending cycle.

Application software

Application software works on top of, and necessitates, all the hardware and networks. Most modern business applications use a client-server model, which means the main software resides on a dedicated server, and the users have a small interfacing program on their desktop computers. Examples are software for CRM (described in the trends section), databases, e-mail, inventory management, sales reporting, and countless examples that are market-specific.

Industry Trends

Evolving occupations

If there's one constant of technology and tech careers, it's change. Given the speed of technological advancements, some positions may even completely transform or disappear.

Programmers are a good example of this ongoing process. Currently, programming jobs are among the most prevalent in IT. However, one of the most rapidly growing sectors of the computer services industry is pre-packaged software. Also, advances in programming language capabilities allow end-users to carry out many of the duties that programmers traditionally performed. Microsoft's Visual Basic, which creates a graphical environment for users to construct their own programs, is one example.

Transitions in Technology

"There are some people who think that programming will transform dramatically, if not disappear," says Steve Johnson, senior fellow of The MathWorks, Inc., and former board member of the Computer Research Association.

Other positions have already changed dramatically. "Between about 1990 and 1995, the term 'system administrator' meant the person who came in for a shift and mounted tapes to collect data backups. By 1995, it meant the person who was responsible for the global communication infrastructure of the company," explains Johnson. "A system administrator may be totally different 10 years from now, because a lot of the things that system administrators do today will be done automatically by the software."

Of course, not every job will change significantly. Support positions like sales and management have remained fairly static. "I think that the basic problems that need to be solved by both of those functions are going to be the same for a long, long time. They still need to understand, coordinate, and lead people, and they still need to talk to customers to effectively identify the customer's needs," says Johnson. However, aside from select support jobs, IT positions typically do not remain the same.

Visit Vault at **www.vault.com** for insider company profiles, expert advice, career message boards, expert resume reviews, the Vault Job Board and more.

V/\ULT CAREER LIBRARY

7

Johnson explains, "Almost everything else is fair game. Even documentation has changed radically. Documentation would have meant books 10 years ago. Documentation now means web pages, and there are documentation people that didn't make the cut."

The economy

The IT field is in a transitional state. It remains relatively lucrative for those holding jobs. However, many factors in recent years have driven down the number of IT jobs substantially, and recovery has been slow.

IT technology is still used in almost every field. Non-IT companies are the major employers of IT positions; in fact, over 91 percent of all IT jobs are in non-IT companies. That's the good news.

While American companies placed over 86,000 IT jobs in the first quarter of 2003, that's nearly 11,000 less IT jobs than were placed in the previous quarter. In fact, demand for IT was lower in the first quarter of 2003 than at any point of 2002.

The bright side is that while demand has lessened, salaries are stable. Only 8 percent of all companies surveyed for this book reported reducing IT salaries and 75 percent say they've raised them.

Still, the overall sense of the technology field's future is cloudy. "Our sense is that it's going to be a fairly low-growth business for the next couple of years," says Brad Smith, Vice President of Research at Kennedy Information. "It isn't a matter of bouncing back to some pre-bubble time. [IT as a field] has fundamentally changed. It's a maturing market. There's a lot more doubt on the part of purchasing customers as to what the payback will be for their investments in software or consultants."

Fewer companies expanding their IT resources means less hiring. "Right now, you can't even get into IT with training. The job market is so terrible. But I think that's cyclic," says Johnson. The cycle may be too slow for the majority of IT jobseekers, however. While some experts predict that the economy will remain slow until 2004, other predictions put recovery even further away. "I would say that at least through 2005, it's going to be low-to-mid, single-digit growth overall," predicts Smith.

Security and the growing virus threat

There's one particularly bright spot in the IT market, however – the need for greater IT security. For instance, in the summer of 2003, a major calamity brought the need for more competent computer network and security people to the foreground.

The Microsoft Corporation's flagship product, the Windows computer operating system, has been the most popular and prevalent operating system in the world. Even the U.S. armed forces use Windows computer networks. And, on July 15, 2003, a new federal agency, the Department of Homeland Security, announced that it had awarded Microsoft a five-year, $90-million contract to supply the software for about 140,000 of the department's most important desktop and server computers.

But the next day, July 16, 2003, Microsoft issued a security bulletin admitting that a major security flaw existed for nearly all versions of Windows. The flaw could allow hackers to access and utilize other computers that used Windows. Within the next month, several viruses took advantage of this flaw, attacking computers around the world.

The viruses spread with more speed and destruction than any other previous computer virus. MessageLabs Inc., a company that filters e-mail for corporate clients worldwide, announced that it intercepted over one million incidences of the "Sobig.F" computer virus on August 20th, meaning that one in every 17 e-mail messages that the firm scanned was infected. The company had never intercepted that many incidences of a virus in a single day. It became clear that most companies' network systems were not capable of withstanding such virulent attacks.

By August 21, 2003, the Symantec Corporation, which produces the Norton AntiVirus software, declared the latest worms to be a severe threat to all computer users. Symantec had received reports of severe disruptions on the internal networks of many large enterprises, including Air Canada and the U.S. Navy and Marine Corps. Symantec upgraded the worms to a Category 4 risk, one level below the most severe risk category.

"For network security, because it's such a new field, the concept really wasn't understood until recently," says Tracey Losco, Network Security Analyst at New York University. "With viruses getting more and more media coverage, more and more people are aware of them."

The U.S. government has recently developed NIPC, the National Infrastructure Protection Center. NIPC is a division of the Department of

Visit Vault at **www.vault.com** for insider company profiles, expert advice, career message boards, expert resume reviews, the Vault Job Board and more.

VAULT CAREER LIBRARY

9

Homeland Security that deals solely with electronic security, focusing on Internet security and electronics communications. And, of course, the government is not alone in the need for better security. Companies today generally use networks and the Internet to sell their products and communicate with customers. The upshot – a bright market for IT security work.

Open source vs. Microsoft

People entering IT discover that there are two general computer paths to follow. In a nutshell, there are software applications, systems, and database programs that work on computers using Microsoft Windows, and then there is "open source" software. Open source programs are free software that any user can modify and redistribute. Open source software and Microsoft software look different, act differently, and are operated very differently from each other. IT people must generally learn at least something of both. But, when starting out, it tends to be easiest to choose one path from which to learn the basics. However, the popularity of both tends to fluctuate.

Microsoft products dominate the software market; about 90 percent of all home and business computers use the Microsoft Windows operating system. An overwhelming majority of computers are sold with Microsoft products already installed. However, open source resources have been spreading in business because they do not cost anything, they have a reputation of speed and reliability, and they give users a great deal of power to tailor the products to their own needs.

Linux is an open source computer operating system, usually used in server computers. Server computers power both web sites and e-commerce transactions, and they enable large-scale database applications, filing, and printing tasks. With so many businesses modernizing, demand for server computers constantly grows.

Many companies decided to start using Linux after its release in 1994 because of its low implementation cost and its highly configurable nature. In 1999, Linux became the second most popular server operating system behind Microsoft's NT server. In 2000, computer chip maker Intel, the Internet company Netscape, and two venture capital firms invested in Red Hat Software, the foremost distributor of Linux.

Major computer manufacturers have also been supporting Linux. Today, IBM uses Linux to power its entire server product line. Dell sells laptop, desktop, and server computers equipped with the Red Hat brand of Linux.

Hewlett-Packard and Gateway use several brands of Linux for their computer products. Network software maker Novell Inc. is also beginning to cater to the growing popularity of Linux. Novell, which already ships networking software for Windows and its own Novell NetWare operating systems, now distributes its networking software for Linux network servers.

However, open source services do have drawbacks.

"When I'm using open source resources, I'm responsible for everything about them," says John Running, the founder of MobiusWEB, an IT consulting firm. "The great thing about Windows is that someone else is responsible for them. They have all kinds of security problems, but Microsoft is always putting up patches." When a company services many clients, the company typically does not want to worry about finding security holes in the software it uses.

Such reasons may explain a recent business migration from Linux. From May to July 2003, Microsoft saw a 300 percent increase in the number of web sites (88,400) hosted by their Windows Server 2003 software. Five percent of those sites using Server 2003 switched from Linux. Forty-two percent of those sites are new sites.

But another open source operating system, BSD, may soon turn the trend back towards open source. BSD is the only other server operating system besides Windows and Linux that continues to add users. In July 2003, nearly four million hostnames, including Internet giant Yahoo.com, used BSD. Apple Computer's latest operating system, OSX, also uses a version of BSD.

Lawsuits aplenty

Microsoft, the second-largest U.S. company in terms of stock market value, has been sued several times for alleged anti-trust law violations. For instance, AOL recently sued Microsoft, claiming that the software giant used illegal tactics to ensure the dominance of Microsoft Internet Explorer over AOL's free Netscape web browser. Netscape browsers are based on the open source Mozilla browsers. In May 2003, Microsoft agreed to give AOL $750 million, as well as a royalty-free, seven-year license of its browsing technology, to settle the suit. Microsoft will also provide technical information to AOL to ensure that its products can run effectively on Microsoft's Windows operating system.

Visit Vault at **www.vault.com** for insider company profiles, expert advice, career message boards, expert resume reviews, the Vault Job Board and more.

VAULT CAREER LIBRARY   11

SCO vs. IBM

In March 2003, the SCO Group, which inherited the intellectual property rights to the Unix operating system, sued IBM for over $1 billion. SCO claimed that IBM inappropriately extracted confidential and proprietary information from Unix and used it to build Linux. Analysts said that SCO's move was an act of desperation, since SCO had not been profitable. Although many experts and members of the Linux community remain skeptical that SCO will succeed, the suit, with its huge implications, gained the attention of the entire IT community.

In June 2003, SCO increased the amount of damages sought to $3 billion. In August, SCO revealed licensing prices it would charge companies for using Linux. Although Linux can be downloaded for free, and Red Hat Inc. sells desktop Linux for $39, SCO announced it would charge users $199 for the right to use desktop Linux, and $1,399 to use Linux for servers. Linux users will have to pay up or face a legal battle, if SCO wins this IBM suit. If Linux is not free or inexpensive, it loses a huge advantage in the market with Microsoft.

Linus Torvalds, the creator of Linux, said that the allegedly offending Linux code is actually a part of the BSD operating system, and not part of the originally copyrighted Unix code. Many other members of the open source community have challenged SCO to show the offending code under a non-disclosure agreement, confident that the suit's claims cannot hold up to scrutiny. Nevertheless, if SCO prevails, Linux development would be hindered, and the general public would have a difficult time obtaining the expensive and privately owned operating system. Any company using Linux would be affected.

A win for SCO would affect the IT industry of many countries. The IT industries of developing nations use low-cost Linux extensively. Open Source Victoria, an open source marketing, advocacy, and focus group in Australia, filed a complaint with the Australian Competition and Consumer Commission, asking them to investigate SCO's activities. Open Source Victoria claimed that SCO's suit threatens hundreds of thousands of Australian users of Linux.

Although the effects of this suit could be widespread, other IT suits have been even more aggressive in their reach.

The RIAA

Music copyright infringement has become a major topic in the IT industry. In fact, the RIAA (Recording Industry Association of America), which produces 90 percent of the music recorded in the U.S., had obtained 900 subpoenas in federal courts in the summer of 2003. The RIAA seeks people who use computer programs to illegally share copyrighted song recordings. The 900 subpoenas ordered Internet service providers to disclose information about their customers to the RIAA.

Senator Norm Coleman, R-Minn., said at the time, "This barrage of RIAA subpoenas is creating such a backlog at the U.S. District Court in the District of Columbia that the court has been forced to reassign clerks to process the paperwork."

In one famous case, the RIAA filed suits against four college students for trading copyrighted songs. The RIAA sought $150,000 in damages per song, the maximum allowed by law, for each of the approximately 652,000 songs the students offered to trade, for a total of $97.8 billion in damages.

RIAA senior vice president for business and legal affairs Matthew Oppenheim said he expected the suits to serve as a warning to college officials who have not been keeping track of their networks.

Virginia Rezmierski, adjunct associate professor at the University of Michigan's School of Information and Gerald R. Ford School of Public Policy, says schools that have agreed to monitor their networks have put themselves in a position they cannot fulfill, considering the high number of student web sites.

This means that more and more qualified people will be needed for networks everywhere. Campuses and corporations will need keen eyes on their systems to ensure that employees and students do not trade any copyrighted songs on the networks.

Health care booms

The U.S. Department of Health and Human Services (HHS) developed federal privacy standards for patients, as part of the Health Insurance Portability and Accountability Act of 1996 (HIPAA). These standards, the first federal ones of their kind, protect patients' medical records and other health information provided to health plans, doctors, hospitals and other health care providers. On April 14, 2003, the standards went into effect.

Visit Vault at **www.vault.com** for insider company profiles, expert advice, career message boards, expert resume reviews, the Vault Job Board and more.

VAULT CAREER LIBRARY   13

Among other things, the standards dictate that communications between doctors and patients must be secure. Also, the medical records themselves must be secure, so that they cannot be sold or shared without the patient's permission. The HHS has issued technical materials to explain the privacy rule, and has promised to expand and update the materials to further assist hospitals and doctors to comply. This means most hospitals and health care units must update their office technology in order to manage patient data.

National health care spending stands at around $1.5 trillion, and health care spending growth has outpaced Gross Domestic Product growth since 2000. Many of the industry's IT-hungry companies have been enjoying steady growth for the past few years, including health care companies, hospitals, pharmaceutical companies, health care equipment companies, medical practices, and health insurance companies. Many IT positions in health and allied services are projected to grow by well over 100 percent.

In particular, a few IT positions promise to grow faster than others across every medical category. Computer support specialists, software applications engineers, and network and computer system administrators look to grow by at least 50 percent in every category. Database administrators sit at or near the top of every growth category as well, with their lowest growth projection still at 39.5 percent in the medical instruments and supplies industry.

Many pharmaceutical and genetics companies are experiencing growth. These companies also have demand for project managers, systems analysts, systems architects, computer scientists, and managers. Demand for network security jobs at medical companies is also expected to increase in the next 5 to 10 years.

Working at a health care company can be stressful, and the IT work can be fast-paced and relentless. Dara Sanderson is a programmer gone work-traffic coordinator at WebMD, an information service web site for physicians, consumers, and health care plan providers. "I am literally jumping and hopping from the minute I walk in the door, until right before I leave in the evening. It's fun, because the time flies by, but the pace of work there is just bananas," says Sanderson. "We literally have people publishing new pages, new reports, and new tools every single day, all day long. And because it's medical information, almost everything needs to be medically and legally reviewed before it can go up on the site."

Globalization

Global outsourcing has caused great concern among American jobseekers and jobholders alike. Many major American corporations have begun to outsource their work to "offshore facilities," meaning offices in foreign countries like India. While the trend seems to be continuing strong, there remains a place for the well-trained IT person.

"A company could outsource to India or where-have-you, to get about the same IT job done for a much, much cheaper price," says Roger Moncarz, economist for the U.S. Department of Labor. Experts say that one American employee can cost five times as much as a trained employee in India, and consulting costs can be cut by three quarters by using Indian consulting companies.

In 2000, General Electric's CEO, Jack Welch, announced that GE would outsource 70 percent of its work, and that 70 percent of that work would go to offshore facilities. The sluggish economy has caused major hirers of IT, like Internet and electronics companies, to outsource to other countries since then.

The number of companies outsourcing offshore is not known, because many companies are reluctant to admit the practice. However, according to the ITAA's latest study in 2003, 22% of the large IT companies surveyed admitted moving work overseas. This is three times the number of non-IT companies that admitted moving work overseas.

Dell Computer, Texas Instruments, Philips, Hewlett-Packard, and Bank of America have sent key functions, research, and engineering jobs to India. Companies like IBM and Intel have been outsourcing to India for decades. Microsoft's Senior Vice-President, Brian Valentine, urged department heads to hire offshore in a summer 2002 presentation. And, in November 2002, founder and chairman Bill Gates announced that Microsoft would invest $400 million over the next three years to expand its activities in India.

Many South Asian countries have a low-cost of living, low salaries by American standards (e.g. $5,000 for a starting IT engineering salary in India), and an explosion of Asian college graduates (e.g. the Philippines, which produces 380,000 college grads each year). These factors have begun to entice more U.S. companies to continue the offshore outsourcing trend, which has negatively impacted American IT salaries. Forrester Research predicts the loss of at least 3.3 million white-collar jobs and $136 billion in domestic salaries to lower-cost countries by 2015.

Visit Vault at **www.vault.com** for insider company profiles, expert advice, career message boards, expert resume reviews, the Vault Job Board and more.

VAULT CAREER LIBRARY   15

Backlash has begun against the perceived outsourcing of American jobs. In December 2002, the New Jersey Senate unanimously passed a state bill that would bar all government contracts from being outsourced to foreign countries or workers. Connecticut, Maryland, Missouri, and Wisconsin have been considering similar bills. Groups like the ITAA (Information Technology Association of America) have traditionally been against such bills, fearing that they may be anti-trade in nature.

Despite the outsourcing trend, IT jobs for qualified American workers continue to exist. "I've been hearing for over 10 years that programming is going to become a minimum wage job, because there are all these people in India who are willing to work for nothing. And I haven't seen it happen," says Steve Johnson. "And I think the reason is that, to be good and effective in a company, you need to have domain knowledge. There just aren't that many pure programming jobs. You need to know who the customers are, and you need to be able to adapt what you're doing for the customers. If you get into a situation where you have a pure programming job, then shipping [the work] off to India is a fine thing I guess. But I haven't run into very many pure programming jobs."

Next Generation Technology

Next-generation software development

Programming or "coding," the art of writing computer commands in pseudo-human languages, is at an exciting point in its history. Being a programmer once meant working long, isolated hours in front of a screen, typing away in über-cryptic languages, using software called a "compiler" to ready your work for use, finding your mistakes, and then going through the process over and over again until your project got done, whether that meant it was elegant or just good enough. Modern programmers work as hard as ever, but today there are several trends resulting in happier programmers and better software. Programmers today often work in teams, constantly conducting a form of peer review, and involving customers and partner companies as well – a trend known as extreme programming. Programmers today also have more tools at their disposal than ever before. More and more, object-oriented programming is becoming commonplace; that trend involves the use of pre-written code groups assembled like building blocks and then tweaked to specifications. In still another trend, the concept of application programming interfaces (APIs; the code libraries provided by companies for other companies and large customers to use in custom development) is evolving into APIs that run distributed over wide-area networks such as the Internet. Microsoft's ".Net" initiative is one example of this. Some believe these trends and others are pointing in a direction of self-maintaining software, a concept that itself is part of a trend also applicable to hardware, and called "autonomic computing" by IBM and others.

CTI

"Computer/telephony integration" refers to any technology solution that merges computing with telecommunications. The term is less popular than it was in the 1990s; people today refer to the particular solutions instead (also, "telephony" is pronounced tuh-leff-a-nee, not tell-a-foney). There are at least half a dozen common examples, including those listed below:

- **Speech recognition** –such as when you call to make an airplane reservation and you speak to a computer posing as a human

- **Internet telephone calls** – using a computer network instead of a traditional phone network, in order to save money, also called "voice over IP"

- **Unified messaging** – having all of your e-mail, faxes, and voice-mail reside in a single inbox, accessible by both computer and phone

- **PC-based PBXs** – a PBX is a traditional corporate phone system, but some companies today consolidate the whole contraption onto a single CD running on a server with special phone line attachments

- **Click-to-talk** – chatting with a sales or support agent, via a web site

- **Predictive dialing** – such as when computers known as auto-dialers place several calls from an agent's phone at once, based on an algorithm which assumes that at least one of the calls will reach a live human – when the algorithm guesses wrong and multiple people answer their phones, the agent can only speak with one at a time, so that's why sometimes your phone rings and a computer asks you to hold or simply hangs up on you.

Another major aspect of CTI is CRM ("customer relationship management"), which is the technique of using any combination of these six and other technologies to improve the customer's experience in a cost-saving way for your company.

Visit Vault at **www.vault.com** for insider company profiles, expert advice,
career message boards, expert resume reviews, the Vault Job Board and more.

VAULT CAREER LIBRARY   17

Data management

According to the most recent "How Much Information?" report, five exabytes of new data were created in 2002 (http://www.sims.berkeley.edu/research/projects/how-much-info-2003). Gigabytes (a thousand megabytes) are the standard measure of modern computer storage; it takes more than a billion gigabytes to have an exabyte. That's an incredibly large amount of data – "equivalent in size to the information contained in half a million new libraries the size of the Library of Congress print collections," the report states – and managing it all requires an equally massive amount of technology. Researchers are busy building more efficient ways to do so. So far, they've come up with Extensible Markup Language (XML), three-dimensional databases, and data warehousing, to name a few.

In simple terms, XML is the technique of giving artificial context to Web-based data. Say you and I and your friend all own car dealerships. Maybe you sell Ferrari, I sell Fiat, and your friend sells Ford. Your online data refers to exotics, mine to imports, your friend's to commuter vehicles. It's all the same to a customer's computer when she searches online for "cars" but, because of our specialties, our dealership computers literally don't speak the same language. XML solves that – it tells the customer's search engine that Ferrari, Fiat, and Ford are all categories of the same data. Therefore all of the dealerships get included in the customer's search, and she can then choose the kind of car she's looking for. Three-D databases are much more complicated to explain. Think of a traditional database as information stored on a flat sheet of paper (two dimensions). To add more data, that sheet of paper has to get bigger and bigger, which makes it more tedious and time-consuming to retrieve. By adding a third virtual dimension to a database, you exponentially increase the options for how the data is stored, and you create new kinds of information storage and retrieval options. But regardless of the database modeling method, large data sets are typically organized into virtual warehouses. Data warehousing includes staging (preparing to organize inbound data), data marts (the term for groups of information ready for outbound use), and other terms.

Next-generation networking

Business-class networking technologies evolve at a slower pace than server and storage technologies because of the importance of product interoperability. Whereas home or small-business computer networks transmit data at either 10 megabits or 100 megabits per second, the trend in business networks is to operate at gigabit or even 10-gigabit speeds. Business networks also allow for remote access protected by advanced security features. Another thing distinguishing business networks is modern technologies for managing the data traffic, such as load balancing (as in servers). Load balancing and other traffic management features sometimes are implemented via appliance-like devices that plug into existing networks, but slowly these features are becoming a part of the basic traffic directors (routers) themselves. There are also trends in wide-area networking technologies, such as asynchronous transfer mode and SONET, and there are intra-cluster technologies for moving data directly between computers' memories, such as InfiniBand and others.

Next-generation servers

Servers may look like and even share parts with personal computers, but they have many special features to give businesses better reliability for using so-called mission-critical software. Some examples of server features for high availability purposes include the use of multiple processors and network connections to minimize downtime if something breaks, easy-access panels for maintenance when things do break, and larger and more powerful cooling fans and power supplies. Aside from these business-class features, servers also typically do without consumer features, such as game connectors, fancy exterior cases, good sound cards, floppy disk drivers, and printer ports.

Modern server computers also increasingly use a technology called 64-bit processors, which allow for more data pathways in and out of the computer's brain, compared to desktop-class 32-bit processors. In addition, besides business versions of the Microsoft Windows operating system that dominates personal computers, servers frequently use more powerful but less user-friendly operating systems such as Linux, Solaris, and Unix. In the biggest companies, servers can also take the form of mainframes and supercomputers, which are basically very expensive, special-purpose machines for ultra-high-speed needs. Servers of all kinds sometimes use a technique called virtualization, which can either make one server appear as many, or many servers appear as one. Clustering (the use of a few servers working as a team) is also a significant trend.

Other trends include blade servers and grid computing. A blade is a computer built on a single circuit board, which may forego having its own memory or storage, instead sharing those and other components with a group of blades. The advantage to this approach is increased computing footprint and modularity – that is, you can fit many more blades than traditional servers in the same physical space, and they're much easier to swap out. A grid is a

Visit Vault at **www.vault.com** for insider company profiles, expert advice,
career message boards, expert resume reviews, the Vault Job Board and more.

VAULT CAREER LIBRARY   **19**

more advanced, networked version of a similar concept – that is, many servers and even many data centers across a wide geographic area linked together to share resources. However, both blades and grids have some drawbacks and are still considered unproven technologies.

Next-generation storage

Without data storage technology, you would have to re-enter programs by hand every time you turned on the computer. The vast majority of storage today is of the magnetic variety, pioneered by IBM and 3M in the mid-1950s. The capacity, physical size, read/write speed, and reliability features are exponentially better today, but the basic technology is the same: miniature magnets are electrified to cause a change in polarity, and each one is equivalent to the binary form of the numbers 0 and 1, off and on, that are the lowest levels of computer software. Some uses call for a non-magnetic kind of storage, optical media, which is similar to CDs or DVDs. Regardless of whether the media is magnetic or optical, the storage can also be internal to a server or external in special storage components. These components, themselves part of a massive worldwide industry, involve interconnecting refrigerator-size storage cabinets with complicated high-speed networking technology based on fibre optics, and then linked into the servers. That's called a storage-area network (SAN). Another technology, network-attached storage (NAS), uses similar techniques over more standard Ethernet connections. SAN and NAS each have their place, but they are increasingly converging. Tape storage is the most common way to archive old data for long periods of time. It's not a new trend at all, but what's new is the use of tapes and tape drives configured in a SAN. A new development for data backup is to use low-cost hard drives for selected tape functions. Another new trend is something called object-based storage, which is a software method for ensuring the authenticity of data by giving all data unique ID traits. As with server technology, modern storage systems increasingly use virtualization and clustering technology.

Remote access

In today's IT world, people need data access when they may not be near computers, so mobile communications are vital. To support the technologies such as VPNs (virtual private networks) connected to devices such as handheld computers and e-mail gadgets, IT specialists need to be trained in networking and security. Even from remote computers, remote access is still a challenge due to authentication issues and viruses. One solution some

The Jobs

CHAPTER 2

Careers in information technology roughly fall into several categories: creators, managers, maintainers, and the supporting cast. Creators are people whose job it is to imagine, design, build, and test all kinds of computer products. "Computer products" these days can mean anything from A-bombs to zoological software, but in the IT sense it simply means actual computers, software, and networking technology.

Maintainers are the people who keep computers working so humans can concentrate on doing tasks and solving problems. Maintainers spend most of their time installing, fixing, and upgrading the computer, software, and networks, and in helping non-IT people interact with them. Technology supporters include all the people who work in non-technical roles that are vital to the IT field, such as sales, training, marketing, finance, and law.

As you read about each type of position, keep in mind that IT job responsibilities tend to overlap. The scope of each position varies from company to company.

Creators

If your career ambition is to design, build, or manage new IT products, then you're a creator. You'll mostly likely work for a technology vendor, or perhaps for a subcontractor or large company that has custom IT needs. Among the creators are technical staff and business staff. Key roles among the technical staff are R&D (research and development), designers/developers, programmers, testers/QA (quality assurance) staff, and support. Key roles on the business side include product/project managers, industry liaisons, technical writers, and market researchers/pre-sales engineers.

Research and development (R&D)

R&D professionals are typically either scientists or engineers with a niche specialty. R&Ders study the future of their employer's industry in pursuit of better technology that product designers can eventually turn into commercial successes. In addition to working in a laboratory, they do academic research, online or in traditional libraries. Research and development professionals also keep up to date with knowledge in their industry, attending trade events,

Visit Vault at **www.vault.com** for insider company profiles, expert advice, career message boards, expert resume reviews, the Vault Job Board and more.

V∧ULT CAREER LIBRARY   21

reading prolifically, and cataloging results of experiments. Sometimes the research goal will be a modest improvement in your company's existing technology, and other times the sky's the limit.

A famous example is the story of how a Xerox physicist, Gary Starkweather, invented the laser printer. His job was to come up with small improvements in traditional copiers of the early 1970s, but he realized that the new laser technology could probably carry data bits thousands of times more efficiently than copiers at the time did. He worked on this project in his spare time until his managers told him to stop chasing his foolish laser pipe dream. Finally he convinced management to grant him a transfer to Xerox's R&D department, where he worked full-time on the laser technology. The result was that he fathered a whole industry.

Keep in mind that R&D doesn't have to be as hugely impressive as Starkweather's work to still be important. Sometimes minor but clever developments can make the difference between an IT product that doesn't work and one that changes the world. A well-known example is that of David Bradley, the IBM engineer who in 1981 invented pressing "Ctrl-Alt-Delete" to restart the PC when it crashed. In the laboratory, Bradley's peers restarted computers by short-circuiting them with a screwdriver shaft. Thinking up Ctrl-Alt-Del was a very small task and took just a few lines of programming code, but now it is used in computers around the world.

Designers/developers

Those who work in IT design and development roles are tasked with determining new products to make, based on numerous sources of input, including that of R&D. Whereas R&D staff might work on a project simply because it's good science or cool enough to make a nice corporate demonstration, designers/developers need to concern themselves with what will sell. These employees also need to consider what the company's competition may be working on – the most successful technology is not always the most technically superior technology. Once those decisions are made, designers and developers figure out the course of action needed to turn the idea into a real product. For example, what programming method will be used, and which language will be used? If the product involves hardware, is it better to build something from scratch, or to use off-the-shelf parts? What are the product's specifications, and how static or dynamic do they need to be? These and many other tasks are all the responsibilities of designers and developers.

Systems analysts

Systems analysts ensure that their companies reap the maximum benefits possible from computer technology, IT personnel, and their business procedures. They accomplish this through discussion, goal defining, analysis techniques, and extensive testing. Also referred to as systems developers or systems architects, these analysts may decide to develop completely new computer systems for a company, or to optimize and expand existing hardware and software. A more specific set of these workers, called programmer analysts, design and update systems software. Programmer analysts must know both programming and systems analysis.

Most systems analysts work with computer systems specific to the company's industry. Accounting, engineering, and publishing systems analysts would each work with different computer systems. Analysts often have backgrounds in their companies' fields.

Once hired, analysts first talk to the managers and users to determine the goals of the company's computer system. Then, they determine the exact system problems to overcome.

The analysts determine the computer hardware and software required for the new system, creating specifications for engineers and computer programmers to follow. Once the programmers and engineers create the new system, the analysts supervise tests of system performance. They also work with the programmers to debug systems.

Hardware engineers

Working with computers and computer-related equipment exclusively, these engineers research, design, build, and debug computer hardware. They also supervise the manufacture and installation of computer hardware.

The research, design, and development efforts of computer hardware engineers are mainly responsible for the rapid progress in computer technology. Computer speeds double every 18 to 20 months. To remain competitive, these engineers must continually update their knowledge.

Software engineers

There are two basic types of computer software engineers: applications software engineers and systems software engineers.

Visit Vault at **www.vault.com** for insider company profiles, expert advice, career message boards, expert resume reviews, the Vault Job Board and more.

VAULT CAREER LIBRARY   23

Applications software engineers design, create, and modify computer applications. The applications can be general software programs, useful to varied users, or they can be specialized utility programs. These engineers use various programming languages to create this software, depending on the purpose of the program and the environment of the user. The most common programming languages they use to build the software are C, C++, and Java.

Computer systems software engineers plan and maintain a company's computer systems while considering scalability and growth. They observe and assess a department's computer needs, from hardware and software purchasing, to intranet architecture and construction, to tech staff payroll. Systems software engineers work for companies that design, build, and install computer systems. Because of their positions as product designers, they may serve as primary technical resources for sales and support people.

Good analytical, problem-solving, and communication skills are necessary for success here. Inexperienced software engineers usually start off modifying or debugging existing software. As they gain experience, they may design and develop new software, eventually becoming project managers, information systems managers, or chief information officers. Some experienced engineers create their own independent consulting firms.

For example, let's say Hal the scientist perfects a way to display holographic images in computer monitors. In order to build these, developer Cal needs to make some big decisions. What is the biggest monitor that can be built without the holographic image becoming distorted? What's the flattest and smallest monitor that special holography equipment will fit inside? How will the extra parts affect the monitor's power requirements? Will the monitor require special software to interact with ordinary computer video adapters? What effect will screen savers have on the holographic image? Only when developers solve these problems can the programmers and engineers actually construct the monitors.

Programmers

The people who enjoy actually writing computer code are called programmers (and sometimes other, not-as-nice words). (The commands in a program are often referred to as "code," and writing a program is referred to as "coding.")

Programmers, the stereotype says, are brilliant loners who revel in the man-machine interaction. The reality is that while most are very good at math, logic, physics, electronics, or other fields, programmers were not necessarily computer science majors in college, if they went to college at all – some of the world's best programmers are self-taught. Working with specifications from the designers/developers, programmers need to work quickly, efficiently, and often need to work in teams, whether that suits their personalities or not. Decades ago, companies like IBM supposedly paid some programmers by how many lines of code they wrote, not realizing that the programmer who could accomplish the same task with the least code was actually the better employee! In the hacker generation of the 1970s, the idea of doing a task in as little code as possible became known as "code bumming." Programming today is made easier by the advances in developer tools, but is simultaneously made more difficult by the ever-increasing options and hardware choices that software must interoperate with. Entry-level ("junior") programmers will be assigned to the more mundane and boring tasks, such as checking for bugs. The higher you go up the programming ladder, the more chances you'll have to actually create something from a blank computer screen.

To write a program, the programmer uses one of various programming languages (the language chosen depends on the purpose of the program). He or she uses the syntax of the computer language to type individual commands into the computer line by line. After the programmer has typed a complete set of commands that fulfills the goals set forth by the specifications, she or he then compiles the commands into machine language using a compiler. The resulting product is a program.

Since many programmers may modify or update the same group of code, programmers must usually insert comments in their code so that others can work with it. Programmers may also write manuals and documentation for their programs.

There are two types of programmers: applications programmers and systems programmers. Applications programmers write or modify programs that undertake specific tasks, like a program to track a company's inventory. These programs can also be video games, spreadsheets, and other varied software.

Systems programmers write programs to maintain and control computer systems. They may build or modify operating systems and database systems. They may also build or modify network systems, changing how the network and its computers handle jobs and communicate with peripheral equipment such as printers.

Visit Vault at **www.vault.com** for insider company profiles, expert advice, career message boards, expert resume reviews, the Vault Job Board and more.

VAULT CAREER LIBRARY   **25**

Programmers must usually know more than one programming language and more than one type of operating system. Luckily, since many programming languages are similar, programmers can often learn new languages without much difficulty. Experienced programmers may become lead programmers, eventually becoming managers, or they may move into programmer analyst or systems analyst positions.

For example, let's say the Alaska Adventurers football organization wants to sell software for children to keep track of their trading cards. Judy, the programmer, doesn't just sit at her keyboard and start writing. Instead, she has to decide which programming language is best suited to the project, which she'll determine by factors such as what the program has to do, which languages the Adventurers IT department already owns, which she's most comfortable using, and which work best with similar software from the football league and the trading card manufacturers. And, since the team wants to sell the software on floppy disks, not CDs, she has to make the program somehow fit into a disk's limited storage capacity; in addition, to enable the program to fit on older computers which might not have huge hard drives, she needs to make sure it fits within the arbitrary limit of 20 megabytes. She has to program different versions for Windows and Macintosh computers, and she has to make sure the program code can interact with the Adventurers' web site. Inevitably, when she's finished, the developers and the marketing department will suddenly demand six more features, which may conflict with programming decisions she's already made, so she'll have to go back and rewrite much of the original work.

Quality assurance staff

Working in the QA department are people who really enjoy new challenges, or put more frankly, people who like to break things. The job of a QA engineer is to devise and implement both creative and real-world ways of how a new IT product will be used, and then to figure out how the product can be made to better withstand those uses. For hardware products, this may involve virtual and physical stress testing. For example, if you're working in CTI products, you'll test a software-based phone system for how many calls it can process at once before something goes wrong. You might abuse the server with a hammer, to see how it will withstand impact should the customer's office be the site of a major earthquake. In software, QA is mostly about finding "bugs" – mistakes in the program. In both hardware and software, you also focus on usability; that is, how simple is the product to operate for its intended audience? You will test products quantitatively, using sophisticated measuring tools, and you will test things qualitatively, based on user forums and your experience in whether things just feel right. You will also make sure that the product is compatible with everything your designers claim it is, and you may even read the instruction manual despite your personal expertise in the field, trying to think as a customer would. When a product is finished with its testing and your QA number is put on it, the customer will know that at least one person at the IT vendor was looking out for him. Often the product that is the most reliable will be bought over the one that's least expensive.

Working with customers, you're also in charge (along with the product managers) of the so-called alpha and beta product stages. Alpha refers to an early version of a technology product that's good enough to be used for demonstrating to customers and for testing with other products. Beta refers to an almost-finished but not fully debugged product. Terms such as "release candidate" and stable vs. unstable are also used in reference to an IT product's development status.

Let's say, for example, that Majorsoft Corp. decides that foot pedals, not fingertips, are the future of moving a cursor around a computer screen. So they make a new product, WinToes 1.0, and put Salim in charge of quality assurance. Salim assembles a customer forum and testing group, but he finds problems. When the software doesn't work, the customers tend to press harder on the pedals, but the designers didn't make the pedals strong enough, so the inner levers break. When the programs work properly, the pedals are still a problem, because they tend to get stuck in the depressed or "click" position. Customers are told to move the cursor by rotating the pedals with their ankles, but this causes the software to work too slowly. In the end, most of the customers go back to a normal mouse, even though the R&D department says the foot pedals can be 15% more efficient if used properly. Thanks to Salim, they learn otherwise.

Customer support

The challenge of working in a support role is to be technical enough to really understand the problem, but also enough of a "people person" that neither party gets frustrated or becomes unhelpful. There are many funny stories and even whole books written about poor customer support (and about dumb customers), but that is really the stereotype, not the reality. At most decent technology companies, working in support simply means you're an engineer who likes helping people. Entry-level customer support means being the customer's first point of contact, whether by phone, e-mail, or other contact method. Depending on the complexity of your company's product, entry-

Visit Vault at **www.vault.com** for insider company profiles, expert advice, career message boards, expert resume reviews, the Vault Job Board and more.

VAULT CAREER LIBRARY   27

level staff may actually provide support, or may just help customers get to the right expert. More senior support technicians travel frequently to customer locations, where they work not only on fixing a product but also integrating it with the customer's special needs. Support professionals also help channel consistent customers' problems back to designers and developers, to close the product creation loop.

For example, Christine works in the support department of a company that makes remote access software, primarily for business travelers and telecommuters to get into company networks. She spends her day answering questions from customers and resellers on the phone and over e-mail. Sometimes the questions are the same over and over again, such as IT technicians asking how to reset a lost password, and she patiently recites the procedure from memory. Most of the time, the questions are ones where she has to first ask the caller for information about their configuration and then analyze before answering, such as whether multiple users can share a connection, is their support for Linux operating systems, how network security can be improved, etc. Sometimes the questions are more challenging, and she has to send the call to an engineer.

Sales engineers

The job of a sales (or pre-sales) engineer is to be the technical expert on sales calls and in customer visits. When potential customers ask "Can your product do X?" it's your job to give an authoritative and detailed response – or to tell the customer that you'll research his question and reply. You may also work with the customer's consultant, reseller, or systems integrator to help fashion a specific implementation. As with standard sales employees, your compensation may include a commission. The job does have a challenge you'll inevitably face: as an engineer, it may be your style to answer the customer's technical questions with brutal honesty, which isn't necessarily the best way to sell products. Even if the sale doesn't happen, it's also your job to take the customer's technical feedback back to the designers and developers – was the lack or execution of some feature the reason the customer decided against buying it? It's your job to pay attention to these things. You also may get the customer to share information about rival products.

Example: Erik is a pre-sales engineer at Yellow Business Machines (YBM). YBM makes some very complicated products, so Erik joins the salesmen when they visit big customers. Eventually the customers want to know about YBM's software strategy in more technical detail than the salesman can understand. Erik must walk the fine line between answering the customer's question fully and not divulging too much information about upcoming products. The customer also wants to know how the next version of YBM's computers will work with Majorsoft's databases. Erik hasn't studied this, so he has to ask the developers, who tell him the new YBM computer actually will not work with Majorsoft's products. After that, Erik has to find a way to appease the customer without angering the sales manager.

Product managers

Product managers are in charge of the logistics of a product or product family. If your company makes database software, for example, you'll have to manage the developers and programmers, work with marketing about how to advertise the software, ensure the technical writers are producing the documentation on schedule, manage the partnership and third-party compatibility relationships, and of course, stick to your allotted budget. You'll also have strong influence over which features do and don't make it into the product, what the product's price should be, etc. Product managers (called project managers if you're working on something for internal company use) typically have experience in various jobs such as engineering, sales, or marketing – all skills vital to being a good performer in this role. With experience, you'll be assigned to increasingly important products.

Example: Moon Microsystems builds high-performance computers popular among scientists. With their newest computer, called OptServ, product manager Samantha has many tasks. She has to gather all the data from the developers and sales engineers, figure out whether it's more profitable to sell the product in stores or just on the Web, and determine which advertising and marketing plans to use. She thinks about what kind of documentation to include, what the customer support options should be, and which other companies to establish technical partnerships with. She works with parts suppliers, resellers, and quality assurance testers, and she has to figure out what to tell the computer magazine reporter who said the product is too expensive and won't work.

Industry liaisons

This position is usually found only at large companies. Being a liaison is also sometimes referred to as a "technical evangelist," or by the term "technical marketing." The job involves reaching out to spread the word about your company's technology in a more "viral" manner. You will need a very strong command of your products' technical underpinnings, industry trends, history, and competitive landscape. You'll travel frequently to trade shows, press interviews, customer locations, partner meetings, and user group events. You also may be expected to research and write white papers and serve as your company's representative to various IT standards-settings bodies, which is a serious and time-consuming task.

Example: Mike, a liaison at Nadeau Networks, is the public face of his company to the industry. Every day of the week brings a different responsibility. Monday, he's writing an article known as a "white paper" to share information with the various engineering departments. The article has to be very objective and scientific, but at the same time, it must also talk about the reasons why the company's products are superior. Tuesday, he has a meeting with BSB-N, the big standards body for networking, to discuss how the newest networking technology will be shared. Wednesday and Thursday, he's flying to Orlando to attend a major trade show, where he'll also try to figure out what competitors are building. Then on Friday he has to give a speech to a user group.

Technical writers

Read Dilbert too many times, and you'll think technical writers are completely out-of-touch with the real world. For that matter, read a few electronics manuals, and see the problem for yourself. However, most technical writers are real professionals, not just English majors who couldn't get a better job. The basic duty is to research and author all of the documentation for your company's products. There is much more to it than just sitting in front of a word processor and writing the instruction manual. You'll also master and make extensive use of help-file software, write tutorials, copy-edit the engineering department's technical appendices, work with computer artists for screenshots and photographs, and interact with the outside publishing contractor. So while it's true that many IT documents appear to be improperly translated from Martian, the goal of a technical writer should always be to understand your audience and produce a clear message.

Example: Tina the technical writer is put in charge of creating all the documentation for a new printer. The printer is very different in all aspects from Lexmerk's previous models. First, she has to meet with the developers, to learn what's different about this model and who the target market is. Once she understands, she meets with the quality assurance team, to learn for herself how to use the printer. Then she has to collect all of the technical specifications. When these three steps are done, she can begin writing. There is the primary user manual, which she creates in specialized software, along with the online help files. There is the colorful quick start guide, for users who just want to install the printer now and learn the features later. There is also a technical resource manual, for technicians to use in repairing the printer, and a development guide, which other companies can read to help them make compatible products. Tina also decides to include a DVD, for customers who prefer to see, instead of read about, how the printer works and what its new features are. Another job for Tina is to make sure the advertising includes sufficient technical data, but not so much that the art people get it wrong. On top of all this, she has to make the manuals in multiple languages, and get it all finished and proofread under budget and on time.

Users

"Users" is the IT parlance for customers. Whereas the jobs described above are almost entirely devoted to companies that make IT products, except for programmers who also work at non-technical companies in order to customize their IT needs, the jobs described below summarize the IT positions at organizations that simply make widgets or give advice or run hospitals. There are two main categories of user IT jobs: management and labor. In IT management, you're either an executive or a director, depending on the size of your company. As labor, you may be in charge of everything IT-related for a small business of 30 people, or you may have a very specific role such as network engineer, webmaster, or security analyst for a large corporation.

Management

CIO/CTO

These titles are often used interchangeably. The difference between being a CIO (chief information officer) and being a CTO (chief technology officer) really depends on the size of the company and the type of industry. Some people say CIOs are in charge of internal IT, while CTOs are in charge of external IT. Regardless of your title preference, you are, in fact, in charge of IT. That means you manage the rest of the IT staff, produce and adhere to a budget, explain your important decisions to the CEO, such as which technology to purchase and when to conduct major upgrades, make sure the end users are using their computers in a responsible manner, and generally keep everyone as happy as you can. Between all of these important tasks,

Visit Vault at **www.vault.com** for insider company profiles, expert advice, career message boards, expert resume reviews, the Vault Job Board and more.

VAULT CAREER LIBRARY   31

you'll frequently be pulled aside while you walk the company's halls and asked to fix day-to-day problems, the more serious of which tend to be called "fires." You'll also be in charge of the company's phone and voice-mail system (or PBX).

Example: Tom, the CTO of a telecommunications equipment maker, knows his job is very important: if he steers the company's IT in the wrong direction, it could have a negative impact on telephone systems around the world, and could hurt the company's stock price. His job involves representing the company's technology agenda to the board and the CEO, meeting with the very largest customers to find out what their telecommunications problems are, and being the senior decision-maker for controversial technology subjects, all while determining the hierarchy of his various IT and engineering departments, in order to maintain staffing levels, but at the lowest cost. He also spends a lot of time meeting with top-level sales directors of parts suppliers. Another large part of Tom's job is to read as much as he can about the industry and about competitive technology, and to manage the R&D department.

MIS/IT/Call center directors

Director-level jobs mean you're in charge of one part of your company's overall IT infrastructure. You're the primary hands-on guy. As an IT director, you report to the CIO/CTO, or at smaller companies you're the top level. As a call center director (or "contact center" in more progressive companies), you're in charge of the help desk and any customer service representatives. As with a CIO/CTO, it's also your job to stay aware of new technology and your supplier's competitors, in order to keep your IT at a competitive advantage for your own customers. You'll be the main person called on when those "fires" occur at night, weekends, or other off-hours.

Middle management

Every industry has middle managers, and technology is no exception. About two in five of these managers work in service industries, mainly for computer and data processing services. Insurance and financial services firms, government agencies, and manufacturers also employ many of them. These managers play a vital role in companies today, determining the technological direction of their organizations. They determine personnel and hardware needs, conceive technical goals, coordinate research, design business plans, and direct their companies' computer-related operations.

Computer and information systems managers supervise and assign work to systems analysts, computer programmers, support specialists, and other IT workers. They oversee everything from systems design, to hardware supply, to the development and maintenance of computer networks, to the implementation of Internet and intranet sites. Dealing with both top executives and lower-level employees, they coordinate their department's activities with other companies or non-tech departments.

Example: North American Express, which makes credit cards, has several director-level employees. Two of the most important are the IT director and the call center director. Marc, who's in charge of IT, reports to North American Express' CIO. Marc's job is to directly supervise the IT staff, purchase computers, advise the CIO on the larger, more expensive purchases, and personally fix the biggest technical problems. He also works with Curt, the call center director. Curt's job is very similar – he supervises the customer service and support representatives, and their technology too. He also reports to the CIO, keeps aware of the customer service industry and technology advancements, and communicates with the sales department to help make outbound telemarketing campaigns.

Maintainers

Systems analysts

The role of a systems analyst is to observe large-scale problems and find solutions. Unlike the normal support staff, analysts work on big-picture problems, such as how to make their company's e-mail system in Canada work with their custom inventory system in Japan. That's the kind of problem that can take months to sort out. The analyst does the legwork, keeping in mind the executive's and IT staff's various and sometimes conflicting requirements. In addition to technical problems, analysts also work on ways to save money by using technology – perhaps your Canadian e-mail system works just fine with your Japanese custom inventory system, but how do you know it couldn't work twice as fast at half the cost, if only you made one small change? Analysts use special reporting and charting tools to figure these things out. They also may use "chargeback" tools to ensure that each of the company's departments (IT, marketing, sales, HR, finance, etc). is making the most efficient use of company IT resources and budget.

Visit Vault at **www.vault.com** for insider company profiles, expert advice, career message boards, expert resume reviews, the Vault Job Board and more.

V/\ULT CAREER LIBRARY   **33**

Example: Smith is an systems analyst at New Jersey State Medical Center. The organization includes five hospitals, two universities, and five outpatient centers around the state. As a systems analyst, Smith's job focuses on special projects. He spends his days considering which technologies are the best solutions to NJSMC's problems. He works side-by-side with technicians from the many vendors that supply the statewide healthcare system, and he's the point man for integration projects. He also attends medical technology conferences, helps out the CIO and CTO, and sometimes works hands-on with the IT staff on daily technical issues.

Help desk

Your job is to fix day-to-day IT problems. This is considered an entry-level position, and can be challenging, fun, and a pain in the neck all in the same day. From "How do I double-space?" to "Why won't my screen turn on?" (usually because the user kicked the cord loose!), support technicians – who go by other names as well, such as desktop support, help desk, etc. – need to be patient and true lovers of technology. Even when your officemates' systems are temporarily running smoothly, you'll be busy dealing with panicked workers on the road, facing seemingly easy computer problems that aren't actually that easy, checking IT inventory, installing upgrades and software patches, setting up computers for new employees, organizing the IT room or data center, ordering parts, cleaning out old files from the network, and sundry other tasks.

Example: Couch Corp., the nation's largest maker of home furniture, has a staff of 20 IT support technicians. One of them is Joe. He's a hard-core computer nerd who would spend his free time working on technology even if no one paid him. He has some recurring daily, weekly, and monthly tasks, such as reviewing the reports and logs that Couch Corp.'s servers produce, tuning up employees' computers, assigning equipment such as laptops and cellular phones, and tracking the company's IT inventory. People who encounter commonplace IT problems, such as a Windows crash, lost password, or jammed printer, constantly interrupt his day. He also orders routine supplies, such as backup disks, and teaches Couch employees how to do things like check e-mail remotely.

Network engineers

A network engineer is in charge of all the technology that enables a company's computers to communicate with each other and with the outside world via the Internet. Your day is spent checking and running data wires, installing and maintaining the boxes the wires plug in to (hubs, routers, switches), figuring out why the company's Internet connection is acting slow or is "down", making sure the telecommuting workers have secure access, and paying constant attention to data traffic efficiency by using load balancing and other network management tools.

Example: Chris is a network engineer for a regional chain of auto parts stores. The company is expanding nationally, so it's his job to establish the network connections between each store and corporate headquarters. He spends part of his day making sure the routers and all other physical equipment are working properly. Twice a day he checks the network's traffic flow – if it's too much, the network might clog, and a customer might have to wait too long to return a part – but if it's too little, perhaps it means some important data isn't getting through, or just that the company has too much bandwidth in the first place. He also analyzes the data for any security risks, and he works with the chain's telecommunications providers to make sure they're sticking to the uptime contracts known as SLAs (service-level agreements).

Storage/backup managers

In today's world, storage and backup managers, sometimes called disaster recovery managers, are perhaps the most important of all IT staff. The reason is clear: in case of a man-made or natural disaster, the executives will come looking for you to restore all of the company's data! Buildings can be rebuilt, computers can be replaced, and although we'd rather not discuss this, even new employees can be found – but if your company's business and customer data is lost, it is lost forever. In a privately owned company this is merely an internal problem, but at a public company, executives can actually go to jail for not complying with data retention laws. Moreover, the technology enabling data storage and backup is fairly complicated to use and expensive to purchase. Your company may not experience a disaster on any regular basis, but you certainly will face problems such as crashed computers, lost disks, and broken e-mail systems, and in all of those cases you're responsible for retrieving the proper data as quickly as possible. A huge part of this job is making sure your data backup software is doing its job every night – sometimes you aren't aware of flaws in the backup system until you need to retrieve something, and then it's too late to fix it. But every day there is more data to back up than the day before.

Example: PlayNow, a New York City manufacturer of playground equipment, hires George as its new storage administrator. The company always stored its product designs and database on a traditional server, but now that the company is growing so fast, George must decide what kind of external IT storage is appropriate. Do they want storage that's good at web site transactions, or storage that's best for archiving the actual product drawings? How will PlayNow recover from the flood in its Florida office – did George have a remote backup system in place? How will he decide what data is more important when the files to backup each night exceed the amount of time available?

Database administrators

Every company has a database, and the bigger it is, the harder it is to maintain. The database is the software used for keeping track of customers, parts, sales, partners, inventory, suppliers, and the like. Every entry in a database is called a field (such as a phone number); every group of fields is called a record (such as a customer's full history); every group of records is a table (such as all of the customers in Florida). Because a company's database contains such important information, you will probably have (at least) two copies of everything, mainly a "production" server and a "test" server. When you make important changes to the database, first you'll put them on the test server, and then if all is well you'll update them to the production server. As a database administrator, or DBA, you will also spend much time running data queries on behalf of other company employees – after all, the ability to get intelligent information out of it is why your company uses a software database instead of old-fashioned paper and file cabinets in the first place. To run these queries you will need to master a special kind of programming, such as Structured Query Language. Another task you'll have is making sure the database management software is working properly with your company's other software. For example, every time a customer buys something from your company's web site, that data needs to go into the database. Your company might even have different databases for different tasks, which means you'll have to master different commands and interfaces as well. People who want to be DBAs should understand relational database concepts. They should also learn to anticipate users' needs to logically plan data architecture. DBAs must have good multi-tasking and communication skills, and experienced DBAs may eventually become managers or chief technology officers.

Example: The University of Central Idaho administers all of its academic and tuition records on a massive database management system, known in the industry as a DBMS. Adam is UCI's database administrator. His typical day involves three overlapping tasks. One is to make the database as efficient as possible. Large databases are organized in sections called tables, and he has special software for making sure the hundreds of tables are stored in the smartest possible way, but without sacrificing speed or security. Another big part of his job is to process information queries from professors and from UCI's office workers. For example, if the history department assistant needs to know how many of the upperclassmen from Pennsylvania have a certain grade point average, she'll e-mail the query to Adam, who will likely use a tool called SQL (structured query language) to extract the answer. Adam's third task is to ensure that the database communicates properly with UCI's other IT, such as the storage system and web site.

Telecom technicians

At big organizations, there is usually an IT person (or a team) in charge of the telephone/voice-mail system. The job is to install phones for new employees, make sure the voice-mail system is running smoothly, install and maintain fax machines or fax software, monitor for improper or excessive employee use of the phone system, provide support for telecommuting and traveling workers, maintain the accounts and batteries for the company's cellular telephones and pagers, and work with your company's telecommunications provider(s) and network engineers to ensure that Internet access is running properly and securely.

Example: Chuck is the telecommunications technician for Ticketmonster. Ticketmonster's agents take phone calls all day long, new agents are constantly being hired, and the company has several different phone systems at different locations, including overseas. In addition to the significant task of making sure the offices are all connected to the Internet, Chuck's main job is to keep all the phone extensions working. He also spends time tweaking the voice-mail system and the auto-attendant (which is the beast that makes you press 1 for tickets, 2 for help, or 3 to wait an hour for an uncooperative operator). He works with network engineers and the call center director.

Security specialists

These experts are responsible for both IT and so-called "social" information security. In IT security, you will install and maintain hardware/software combinations for protecting passwords, encrypting corporate data, and securing the network (along with the network engineers) from both internal and external unauthorized users. You'll also make sure all of the company's software has the latest security updates from the vendors. In physical/social

Visit Vault at **www.vault.com** for insider company profiles, expert advice, career message boards, expert resume reviews, the Vault Job Board and more.

VAULT CAREER LIBRARY   **37**

security, you'll make sure the company's employees have the proper identification badges, keep track of any electronic or biometric security technology your company may use, such as closed-circuit cameras and fingerprint scanners, and keep employees aware of issues like how to choose the best passwords and what to say or do if intruders appear on-site or even via telephone or e-mail. As with storage/backup managers, you may not know there is a problem until the problem is already exploited.

Example: First Bank and Savings of Texas recently had some customer accounts compromised by a security breach, so the CIO quickly hired Kevin, an IT security expert. Kevin, in his first week on the job, found all kinds of problems to fix. There were passwords taped to monitors, wildly inconsistent authentication policies at the bank's branches, and a six-year-old web site that any teenager could break in to. His solutions included making every employee pick a new and harder to guess password, establishing a very strict set of security guidelines for the branches, with a punitive system in place for those who disobey it, and a total online makeover with the latest security protection. Every employee also was directed to participate in a security seminar, and all customer data was encrypted.

Programmers (internal)

Unlike the programmers at technology companies, described above, the job of a programmer as a customer's organization is to tailor the software to their specific needs. If you work at a big company, you may be dealing with older software that is no longer made (known as a "legacy" product). That means writing new programs can be a huge challenge, and your skills may not be easily transferable. If your company merges with another company, then you may write software to enable each firm's IT to work together. You may also write software in conjunction with your company's webmaster and other IT staff. You will spend much of your time tweaking existing programs and making minor upgrades, whereas being a programmer at a computer vendor means making more code from scratch.

Example: Brenda is an internal programmer at a defense aerospace contractor. Because of the nature, size, and secrecy of the business, her day involves writing custom programs to allow all of the company's software and tools to work together. She also has to write code that interacts with the assembly line robots, and she has to do it all in several different programming languages. To help, she's built a personal library of code over the years, so she can easily insert modules into a program without having to rewrite something that was already solved six months ago.

Webmasters/web developers

You are the head of the company's web site and its related technology. From fixing broken hyperlinks to engaging in very complicated programming, from interacting with the corporate database to figuring out how to make every web page work just a little bit faster, this role makes the Web your domain (pun intended). Numerous special software and programming languages arose throughout the 1990s to permit all of the emerging web technology to work. Today the Web is a tool, not a toy, and it's your job to make sure the tool is used correctly. The job is not as glamorous or respected as it was in the dot-com heyday, but it's just as important.

Example: Warren is employed by a large independent supermarket. The store carries thousands of products, which constantly change, as do their prices. He has to play the role of art director for the homepage, making sure it's not too hard to read, but still has all the information a customer might want, such as directions, hours, and inventory. He also works with database administrators and network engineers to facilitate customers' online shopping, and so wholesalers can see what needs to be delivered and when. Warren also spends a lot of time editing (to make sure the prices' decimal points are all in the right place), and writes programming code for contests and special promotions. Besides all that, he makes sure the site loads quickly and is accessible from all the major search engines.

Generalists

At small businesses, there often is no CTO, analyst, support technician, network engineer, storage manager, etc. – there is just you, the computer guy, the Jack of all trades, master of no one. As exciting as modern roles like a security manager or webmaster can be, some people prefer being the lone IT employee of a small company. Doing so ensures that your job is different every day and that you're always in charge (of yourself). As the official IT guy at a small company, there is no room for career advancement, but the good news is that small companies will be motivated to keep you on board.

Example: Li works in IT for a small magazine publisher of 50 employees. She is the company's only technology worker, so her hours are numerous, and no two days are ever the same. The IT room has most of the same parts as that of a company 100 times its size – servers, storage, a network. The servers run Linux, most of the employees use Windows computers, but the art department uses Macintosh, so she has to be fluent in repairing all three platforms. She also has to be the webmaster, programmer, telecom

Visit Vault at **www.vault.com** for insider company profiles, expert advice, career message boards, expert resume reviews, the Vault Job Board and more.

VAULT CAREER LIBRARY

39

technician, support representative, and purchaser. While Li's job is stressful, she also has good job security – she's irreplaceable.

Supporters

We've covered the IT jobs at companies that make technology and at companies that use technology. The final category is IT-related jobs – the "everything else" part. As excitingly nerdy as IT is, it's still a business that needs to turn a profit. That is where resellers, systems integrators, consultants, trainers, marketing, accountants, and even lawyers come into play.

Systems integrators

These specialists are hired by customers to make new IT products work with existing ones. Systems integrators embark on projects that take days, weeks, or months to complete. The job is challenging because a customer may wish to integrate IT products that were never intended to work together. Sometimes you'll use off-the-shelf technology to solve a problem, but many times you'll have to custom-build a solution. You'll also have to work with the technology manufacturers, who may or may not have any desire to help you, except to tell you to advise your client to buy more of their products. For many engineers, being an SI is the ultimate challenge, because much of your job description is to make IT work in new ways – essentially to outsmart the original creators.

Jose is an SI specializing in accounting software. Unlike a consultant, who typically just sells advice, Jose's job is to go hands-on inside his client's IT rooms and actually help to design and install solutions. His time in the field with each client can be just a few hours, or even a few months. Once a system is installed and working, the client may keep him on retainer, or they may hire him to train the internal staff.

GETTING HIRED

Education for Tech Careers

CHAPTER 3

Pre-college Preparation

As you grow from childhood pursuits to seriously considering an IT career, spend your pre-college years exploring your interests. If you're teaching yourself to program in a language like C++ or Javascript, or even something simpler like HTML (hypertext markup language, for building simple Web pages), the best way to learn more is to experiment as much as possible. The worst that can happen is your program won't work. Even if your goal isn't to be a programmer, all that hands-on time will inevitably lead you to learn the whole system.

Anther great way to learn on your own, with a little help from friends, is to get involved with real-life or online user groups. General-purpose computer user groups are somewhat obsolete, but specialty groups are very popular, both real-life and online. For example, there's a non-profit organization called Boston User Groups Inc. (www.bostonusergroups.com), which includes more than 50 specialty groups. The meetings usually include snacks, a guest speaker, and hands-on instruction. The online equivalent is the so-called "newsgroups" through google.com. The downside of online groups is the huge amount of spam and other junk you have to wade through, though some groups have volunteer moderators to help reduce this. Of course, an upside to in-person groups is that you're making contacts for future employment. (See the Appendix for a list of some national user groups.)

As fruitful as independent high-tech experimenting and online collaboration can be, it's just as helpful to read extensively. Read every computer magazine, book, and technical web site that you can find. A great example of how successful reading can be: the story of Apple inventor Steve Wozniak. "Woz," as he's known, used to send letters to computer vendors asking for their instruction manuals to computers he could not afford. Then he would sit alone and write programs on paper, based solely on the manuals! That's a bit extreme, but it shows what reading can lead to. (See the Appendix for some reading material.)

College Programs

Jobseekers looking to enter the IT field must nowadays be armed with the proper college degree. Of course, finding an IT job is not as simple as acquiring a computer degree. The right college education must be part of an overall, sensible plan if it is to give you the proper edge in finding an IT career. But an undergraduate education is a good place to start. Many colleges today are re-integrating computer science with its roots in physics and other sciences – and with courses in art, business, and writing.

College, especially a traditional four-year school where you live in a dormitory, is the best time of your life to expand your brain beyond just learning about drinking games. If you learn to think analytically, no matter what the field, you can apply this skill to an IT career. College also provides unique opportunities for peer challenge – that is, separate from any formal clubs or user groups, you'll inevitably become friends with other computer science students. Over lunch and just hanging out between classes, you'll find that conversations stray as much into "What if there were a way to make the computer do this..." as they do into social lives. With the current explosion of ubiquitous Internet access and connected gadgets such as MP3 players and gaming devices, the prospects of what you might brainstorm in the hallways or the cafeteria are very exciting. It happened when Marc Andreessen and others wondered about making a graphical interface for text-based browsers – and formed Netscape; it happened when Sergey Brin and Larry Page wondered about better search engines – and formed Google. So if you want to be a billionaire, make the most of college!

The value of a degree in your job hunt

"It used to be that if you were out of high school, and you got yourself a certification, you could get a job in IT. And obviously, those days are over," says Roger Moncarz, economist for the U.S. Department of Labor. "Now, you definitely need a college degree." IT hiring managers prize four-year college degrees.

In addition to the level of education, the demand for specific degrees has risen. Data pre-dating the dot-com crash "show that a majority of the workers in IT had non-IT degrees. Obviously, there's no reason that we would necessarily expect that trend to continue," says Moncarz. "For the more technical, highly skilled jobs, you probably more need a computer-related degree."

For the more technical IT jobs, like computer engineering, a degree is usually necessary for a jobseeker to be taken seriously. "It's just like anything else. It's like accounting. You can't get out of high school and say, 'Okay, I'm going to become an accountant,' and not have any kind of academic background in it," says Camille Luckenbaugh, employment information manager for the National Association of Colleges and Employers (NACE). "So it's the same with engineers. People who are hiring engineers are hiring them because they need [engineers] for their specific work force."

The main undergraduate IT degrees

To a newcomer, the various 4-year, undergraduate technical degrees out there may look alike. Just like IT jobs themselves, the degree titles may seem similar, and the curriculums of each overlap. However, while each degree has aspects similar to the others, each concentrates on different aspects of hardware, software, and management. Here are the main bachelor's degrees pertinent to technology jobseekers:

- *Computer and Information Sciences:* This umbrella program broadly covers most IT subjects. Students in this program learn about general computing, computer science, information sciences, and information systems.

- *Computer Science:* This degree concentrates on computer design, problems, and interfaces. Specifically, it covers computing theory, principles of computational science, and the hardware design, system design, development, and programming of computers. In addition, it covers a variety of computer applications.

- *Information Sciences:* Students here learn about the theory, organization, and process of IT. This translates into the collection, transmission, and utilization of information, both traditional and electronic. On a more specific level, this program covers the classification, storage, processing, networking, transferring, and signaling of information. This includes courses in systems design, user interface, database development, and related topics.

- *Computer Systems Analysis:* This teaches the principles necessary to select, implement, and troubleshoot customized computer and software systems. Students learn systems analysis, installation, different levels of programming, and debugging. The hands-on side includes the design, installation, testing, and maintenance of hardware and software. Students are also taught how to analyze user

Visit Vault at **www.vault.com** for insider company profiles, expert advice, career message boards, expert resume reviews, the Vault Job Board and more.

VAULT CAREER LIBRARY   **45**

needs, cost-benefits, design specifications, process and data flow, and document testing.

- *Computer Programming:* There are two kinds of computer programming degree programs. One is general, the other specific. The general program teaches students how to design, program, implement, test, and troubleshoot software, in order to drive operating systems. Students are taught both low-level and high-level languages. The specific computer programming degree concentrates on the programming, installation, and maintenance of certain types of software.

- *Computer Engineering:* Students are taught the engineering principles and technical skills necessary to develop and install computer systems. Courses teach computer electronics, programming, systems installation, testing, circuitry, and report preparation.

- *Management Information Systems (MIS):* MIS programs prepare students to create and manage data systems for internal business use. This program also instructs students in how to select and train personnel and how to respond to user requests. Cost/accounting information systems, management control systems, and personnel information systems are taught here. Students also learn about data storage, security, business systems networking, equipment maintenance, and report preparation.

New degrees

In addition to the standard degrees, more specific, IT-oriented degree programs have recently appeared. These programs can help IT jobseekers narrow the scope of their pursuits.

Since such programs are recent, authorities like the Bureau of Labor Statistics do not yet have stats on them in currently released studies, and many of these programs are still rare. "Not many universities offer very specified IT degrees," says Jessica Frias, Recruitment & Technical Coordinator, New York University.

Nevertheless, these programs are showing value. Employers are beginning to notice and look for such programs. "I had somebody from the FBI ask me, 'How come NYU isn't offering a degree in network security?'" says Tracey Losco, Network Security Analyst at New York University. "And he also asked me, 'What are the schools that are offering these degrees?' So, even the government sees that there's a lack in this area."

Below are the main new IT degree programs:

- *Web/Multimedia Management and Webmaster:* Students in these programs learn how to become webmasters and web hosts. This program teaches computer systems, networks, server installation and upkeep, web page creation, Internet security applications, and other related topics.

- *System Administration:* System Administration students learn about computer networks; the hardware, software, and applications for local area networks (LANs) and wide area networks (WANs). This education includes how to put up and take down networks, how to allocate network resources, how to back up network data, how to monitor disk space and traffic load, and principles of information systems security.

- *Web Page, Digital/Multimedia and Information Resources Design:* This program teaches students Internet theory, standards, design, and interface, as well as related topics like web navigation and e-commerce. Students here learn HTML, XML, JavaScript, graphics applications, and other tools required to design, edit, and publish documents, images, graphics, and multimedia for the World Wide Web.

- *Information Technology:* Students in this type of program learn the design of technology information systems, and how various types of businesses use such systems. Courses teach computer hardware and software principles, algorithms, databases, telecommunications, user interface design, and application testing.

- *Data Modeling/Warehousing and Database Administration:* This program teaches students how to create and manage database warehouses and related software programs. On the abstract side, students learn database theory, logic, and semantics. Students also learn how to create database warehouses, how to program database search tools, and other related topics including network issues and security design.

- *Computer Systems Networking and Telecommunications:* Training students to become network specialists and managers, this program instructs in the design, implementation, and management of

Visit Vault at **www.vault.com** for insider company profiles, expert advice, career message boards, expert resume reviews, the Vault Job Board and more.

V/\ULT CAREER LIBRARY

47

networked hardware and related software. In addition to network theory, network configuration, and network management, courses teach security, operating systems, programs, systems design, and systems analysis.

• *System, Networking, and LAN/WAN Management:* Students enrolled in this program learn how to manage entire networks and computer systems. Courses teach LAN and WAN management, system upgrading and diagnosing, and related topics like performance balancing, redundancy, and system maintenance budgeting.

• *Computer and Information Systems Security:* This degree incorporates knowledge on diagnosing security needs, recommending solutions, and implementing security for a computer system and network. Students learn computer architecture, systems analysis, programming, networking, security system design, and related topics like telecommunications, cryptography, and user access issues.

The security degrees are in demand but very rare. "There aren't many institutions that offer them," says Losco. "We're going to move forward [creating these programs] for the public sector. But, so far, there aren't a lot of schools. I could count them on two hands, how many universities have degrees in security." Specifically, Purdue University, University of California Davis, George Mason University, Iowa State University, University of Idaho, Stanford University, Carnegie Mellon University, Georgia Tech University, and James Madison University (Master's only) are some of the top schools that offer this program.

• Computer Hardware Technology: This degree program teaches students the engineering principles and technical skills necessary to help engineers design computer system hardware. Courses teach the architecture, processors, systems design, electronics, and manufacturing processes of computers. This program also covers related topics like testing equipment and computer peripherals.

• Computer Technology/Computer Systems Technology: Students learn to support professionals who use computer systems. This program teaches computer design, architecture, programming, maintenance, and diagnosis. Students also learn report preparation and software repair.

Matching the Degree to the Job

In the job hunt, any bachelor's degree is usually better than none. For some positions, the bachelor's degree does not have to be in a technical field, but employees still want to see applicants with degrees nonetheless. Of course, certain computer-related degrees are usually more useful than others for each particular IT position.

Below are the IT positions and the typical degree requirements for each. If no particular degree is specified, an MIS is the default.

Computer hardware engineers: Even entry-level hardware engineering jobs require an engineering bachelor's degree. Starting salaries for degree holders are higher here than in other fields.

Computer software engineers: Computer science or other software engineering degrees are useful for positions in applications software engineering. For systems software engineer positions, computer science or other computer information systems degrees are useful. The software engineering field often requires broad knowledge of various software programs, and graduate degrees are preferred for senior positions.

Computer programmers: In 2000, over 60 percent of computer programmers held at least bachelor's degrees, usually computer science degrees. If candidates do not have degrees in computer science or information systems, they can supplement their educations with computer courses to become more marketable.

Systems analysts, programmer-analysts, and database administrators: Bachelor's degrees in computer science, computer engineering, information science, or management information systems (MIS) are useful for these positions. Applicants with a bachelor's degree in computer science, computer engineering, information science, or MIS will gain a similar advantage if they have real-world experience behind their degree.

Computer and information systems managers: Employers usually require computer and information systems management employees to hold a bachelor's degree, although employers usually prefer graduate degrees.

Computer support specialists: For the most basic positions, any degree will do. Certain jobs require a bachelor's degree in computer science or information systems.

Visit Vault at **www.vault.com** for insider company profiles, expert advice, career message boards, expert resume reviews, the Vault Job Board and more.

VAULT CAREER LIBRARY　　49

Systems administrators: Although computer-related degrees are not always required, they are a big plus.

Technical writers: College degrees in communications, journalism, English or a technical subject are usually required. Some colleges offer courses or even majors in technical writing.

Sales engineers: Employers require a bachelor's degree in engineering, and previous engineering work will help greatly.

Internships and Cooperative Education

Degree programs also give IT jobseekers the opportunity to take part in internships and cooperative educations. "Internships and co-ops are the most common ways that students gather work experience," says Camile Luckenbaugh of NACE. "And [they are] certainly very highly rated by employers."

These programs allow a potential IT worker to prove she or he can add value to a company. This is invaluable to employers at both non-IT companies and at IT firms. "They're looking for people with demonstrated experience and success," says Brad Smith, vice-president of research of Kennedy Information/Consultant Magazine.

"As a matter of fact, employers not only want to see people with this kind of experience, but they also go to their [own internship and co-op] programs to bring in new hires," says Luckenbaugh. "So, many employers will look to their internship program or co-op program and they'll try to convert those people that they feel are good conversions into full-time employees. They'll convert those people, and then they'll go out and they'll do their recruiting at the college campuses. So, they're extremely important."

In order to obtain an internship, the student should search for good and suitable internship programs. There are many places to search for internships online, but any university career services office should have updated, local internship lists. The student should formulate lists of companies with good internships, noting application deadlines and prerequisite requirements. Then, he or she should research the companies with suitable internships. While large technology companies do offer internship programs, most IT work is still in non-tech companies. Thus, the student should also expect to find a large number of IT internships at non-IT companies.

The student should also bring his or her resume to a guidance counselor or to faculty (at appropriate, IT-related departments) in charge of internships. Due to labor laws, most internship programs will only take students who receive college credit for their internships. The student should show the faculty a structured plan and learning objectives for the internship. Then, the faculty will decide if the student should be awarded college credit for the internship. Once credit is offered, the student and staff can work together on the resume, cover letter, and interview practice.

Students who want to get an internship should show their faculty a scholastic aptitude, an interest in learning new things, and good communication skills. Computer experience and having taken technology classes help as well.

During an internship, students should try to get to know the hiring managers and find out more about the company and its products, in addition to learning about the business and the technology. Doing so will give students an advantage when they want to turn the internship into a job.

The salary outlook for college grads

By and large, IT salaries have remained stagnant. And some grads with computer-oriented degrees are suffering the effects of the slow economy. The expected salaries for many IT graduates are falling.

While most business (economics and finance) grads are enjoying higher salaries this year over last year, technology-oriented business grads are seeing lower salaries this year. The average salary of an MIS grad in 2003 was $40,915, a 4.2 percent decrease from 2002.

The salaries for grads with other IT-related degrees are also down. Computer science grads in 2003 got offers averaging $47,419, which is a 4.4 percent drop from 2002. Information sciences grads received offers averaging $39,787, a 6 percent drop from 2002.

On the other hand, computer engineering students are a hot commodity. "When I look at their salary data compared with other majors' salaries, again, I think that they're holding their own," says Luckenbaugh. Computer engineering grad salaries are averaging $51,720, a 0.3 percent increase over 2002. "We asked [employers] what majors they're going to be hiring. Three

Visit Vault at **www.vault.com** for insider company profiles, expert advice, career message boards, expert resume reviews, the Vault Job Board and more.

VAULT CAREER LIBRARY   51

different engineering disciplines fell into that top ten," says Luckenbaugh. "Electrical, mechanical, and computer engineering." This outlook also seems to be a stable one. "It's probably only been three years that we've specifically said, 'Tell me which degrees you're going to be hiring this year.' What I can tell you is that, in that limited amount of time, those three have consistently appeared in the top ten."

More education time than career time?

Jobseekers thinking of embarking on a four-year (or longer) educational program should be warned at this point. While getting a college or graduate degree may give you an edge in the hiring field, it unfortunately won't ensure longevity. "I spent seven years in school, and it resulted in a six-year career," says one Nortel Networks engineer who was laid off at the end of 2002.

The field of IT is new. Thus, figures do not yet show which percentage of IT workers stay in the field until retirement. However, the trends so far suggest that the turnover, layoff, and burnout rates are high. The size of the total IT workforce peaked in the year 2000. According to the ITAA, increases in IT employment rates since then have been due to a slowing in layoffs, as opposed to any increase in hiring. More and more IT employees have been placed through internal company transfers, and more IT jobs are moving overseas.

This does not bode well for IT workers who have been laid off or who want to pursue a new and different IT path. Such jobseekers may find the job market an unfriendly place. Since the second quarter of 2002, IT hiring and firing rates have been dropping at nearly equivalent levels.

In addition, jobseekers may be unhappy to learn that their education is not nearly over once they graduate. Engineering technologies become obsolete in anywhere between two and a half to seven years. To keep their skills in demand, IT employees must constantly learn new technologies for as long as their careers last.

This drop in job demand and job security is causing many discouraged IT workers, even those who hold bachelor's and master's degrees, to leave IT entirely. According to a survey by Challenger, Gray & Christmas, 51 percent of job seekers changed industries last year. Although that number has dropped this year, the rate still stood at 45 percent through the first two quarters of 2003. Before committing to a long-term educational path, jobseekers hoping to enter IT should be aware of how short the resulting IT career can sometimes be.

The IT MBA

So you have an MBA and you want to go into technology. Where, if anywhere, can your degree take you?

Despite the lore of 1970s-era computer "hackers" who revolutionized personal computing by working out of garages, many other MBA candidates even then were interested in technology. In the five-year period from 1976 to 1981, Harvard Business School produced Dan Bricklin (VisiCalc), Scott Cook (Intuit), Donna Dubinsky (Palm), and Meg Whitman (eBay), among others. Perhaps your background is similar to Bricklin's – he was a MIT-educated engineer, but he has said that he thought of many core ideas for the electronic spreadsheet while in business school.

Today, working in IT or at a technology manufacturer offers many opportunities for MBAs to advance. Some popular fields within IT for MBAs are consulting, director-level positions, finance, law, marketing, project management, sales and training.

Consulting

Many consultants are former successful technologists who want to share what they've learned with others. With solely IT experience, you can get an entry-level consulting job, which means interfacing with your client's own IT staff about their special needs. Your job is to acquire a detailed understanding of the firm's specific IT needs. With a few years of experience and the addition of an MBA degree, you can open your own consulting firm, and participate in panels at trade shows; this can be good experience for venture capital careers. You can also become an in-house consultant for a very large company, which may involve more deadlines and office politics, but you won't have to worry about finding new customers.

Director-level jobs

If you work for a company that manufactures technology products instead of working in the IT department of another kind of company, your MBA degree will often lead you into a director-level job. For example, you might become the director of printers for a company that makes business technology, or the director of R&D for a military software contractor. As a director, your role would be a notch below the division vice president and a notch above the various product managers. Product managers work on just one thing, but as

Visit Vault at **www.vault.com** for insider company profiles, expert advice, career message boards, expert resume reviews, the Vault Job Board and more.

VAULT CAREER LIBRARY

53

director you'd also be working on a technology group's sales, marketing, manufacturing and other aspects.

Finance and law

Finance and law positions in an IT department or at a technology vendor have some aspects that are unusual compared to work in other fields. You may have to deal with patent issues, foreign employee visas, international licensing laws, legal compliance rules for backing up data, and work with multiple layers of distributors, partners, and resellers. With the addition of an MBA degree, you are in good position to become a company's operations director, or even to get a C-level position if you have extensive sales or technology experience as well.

Marketing

Marketing at a tech company involves dealing with advertising, partners, the press, and anything related to corporate outreach. In technology marketing, more so than in other fields, you will be expected to know quite a bit about the technology in question.

Sales

In sales the job description is very clear: make revenue for the company. With an MBA, you can manage entry-level staff, get the best and biggest clients, get into working with partners and resellers, or even enter the field of "competitive intelligence," which is a nice way of saying corporate espionage.

Training

As an IT trainer, you have many career options. You can work in a classroom setting, manage advanced customer support, become involved with technical writing, educate the sales staff, or work with your company's technology partners. With an MBA degree you can become a manager, and get a title such as Call Center Director or VP of User Experience. Technology trainers with business knowledge can also write books. (You see hundreds of redundant technology books on the shelves of your local Barnes & Noble. Writing them is hard work, but can be financially lucrative.)

C-level

Last, and the hardest job to get, is technology upper management. To become a CIO, CTO, or even a CEO in the technology field, an MBA degree is practically a requirement, especially at large companies. There are a lucky few who become business leaders straight out of core technology jobs (and with a lot of natural talent) – the world's richest person, Bill Gates, never even finished his undergraduate degree. But for normal people, if you want to become an IT business leader, you can't go wrong with an MBA: it will help you close big sales, manage company logistics and do high-level strategy.

Of course, for any of the above fields, getting the degree is not enough. "Get the real-world experience," says Paul Buonaiuto, director of recruiting for Computer Associates International Inc., the Islandia, N.Y. company specializing in business management software. The problem with classroom experience alone, he says, is that "Unless you're really out in the trenches, it's difficult to implement sometimes what you read in a book. Real-world experience I hold in more high regard."

To stand out in the hiring process, the ideal job candidate should also have hands-on technology experience. When a pure MBA interviews in technology, it's also important that they first learn not just about the company's business side, but also about its product lines, competition, and customers. That may sound like obvious advice, but "what's sorely lacking in those folks looking for a job is research skills. It becomes painfully evident in the interview" that they know about stock performance but know nothing about its technology other than what's on the web site, says an insider.

Many candidates start out as technical employees or lower-level managers. For them, Computer Associates, like many companies, will pay for a portion of the MBA education. There are a wide range of choices in terms of completing the degree – a traditional MBA program gives you the recognition that business is business and profits are profits, regardless of your industry, while a specialized technology MBA program (such as in e-commerce or systems management) will make you stand out, but can be risky if your chosen specialty market has a downturn. Magazines like *Computerworld*, *BusinessWeek*, and *U.S. News & World Report* sometimes publish features dedicated to ranking graduate programs.

Visit Vault at **www.vault.com** for insider company profiles, expert advice, career message boards, expert resume reviews, the Vault Job Board and more.

VAULT CAREER LIBRARY

55

Certifications

When certifications are useful

Certifications can give jobseekers an edge. They can prove to employers that a candidate has a definite set of skills, and that he or she has had experience working with particular technologies. In a tough job market, any edge helps.

"I think that one thing that's certainly true in the job market today is that companies are not interested in hiring somebody so they can train them," says Steve Johnson, Senior Fellow of The MathWorks, Inc. and former board member of the Computing Research Association. "And I think that very narrow courses, like certification in a particular product, can be a way for somebody to not only get in the door, but also to convince themselves and the company that they have skills that will help the company in the very short term."

"Certifications would be good for somebody who's trying to hop over from a non-IT career," says Tracey Losco, a network security analyst at New York University. While a jobseeker may learn certain languages or skills from a book, a certification forces a candidate to gain "a better insight; the big picture."

According to a survey by the ITAA, employers prize certifications as the third most important applicant qualification. About a third of survey respondents reported that they considered certifications important: 39 percent of IT firms and 32 percent of non-IT firms.

Depends on the position

Of course, certain positions take certifications more seriously than others. The importance of one "will always depend on the type of IT job," according to Jessica Frias, Recruitment & Technical Coordinator at NYU.

Certifications become especially important in networking jobs, because systems and networks form companies' technology infrastructures. Candidates here must show a definite aptitude. "All of the Microsoft certifications, such as MCP, MCSE, and MCSA etc. are great for networking types of positions," says Frias.

In security positions, the need for certifications increases. Competent security is becoming even more critical than ever for any company with technology. Losco emphasizes, "with September 11th, people are more aware of any type of threat now. And I think that [network security issues have] been given more media coverage."

Before jumping into a security course, however, the applicant must figure out whether or not an employer will take a particular certification seriously. Losco says that in network security, "there are only really two big ones that are well-respected."

Certification programs

One type that employers respect is the CISSP, or Certified Information Systems Securities Professional. "It's a good certification because it gives you a broad overview of each part of what a network security professional will do," says Losco. It covers everything from "perimeter defense to actual computer-related security. So it runs the gamut."

This is an example of how a certification can give a jobseeker a useful, broad perspective and skill range. The CISSP will teach a candidate perimeter defense "in the sense of actual building security," says Losco.

"Think of Homeland Defense. Think of what someone would do, if they had a huge computer holding all the financial information for the SEC. And that computer is kept in such-and-such a building. What you have to think about ahead of time is who has access to the building. Are there any doors that are left open in the building? A lot of people think, 'we need to protect the network as much as possible,' but they don't think, 'the cleaning guy leaves the back door open for a good hour every single night, and anyone could just walk in and get physical access.'"

While such a problem is a higher-level disaster planning or disaster recovery issue, it is still included in a network security employee's responsibilities. "It's definitely included," stresses Losco.

Employees also take certifications from the SysAdmin Audit Network Security Institute (SANS Institute) seriously. "They've really been the quickest to get up to speed on [new security issues]," says Losco. SANS courses focus "on digital security and information security, on their vulnerability analysis, and on training people in what they need to look for to secure their machines. How they can secure their machines, how they would know if they've been broken into, and how they can tell from network traffic that they're under attack."

Visit Vault at **www.vault.com** for insider company profiles, expert advice, career message boards, expert resume reviews, the Vault Job Board and more.

V∧ULT CAREER LIBRARY   **57**

SANS offers the GIAC, or Global Information Assurance Certification. As the course description says, students are required to complete a "written practical assignment to demonstrate their mastery of the subject matter. Successful practicals are posted to the GIAC list of certified students (http://www.giac.org/cert.php), both to demonstrate graduates' knowledge and to further educate the community." This gives employers much more information about a candidate than a mere test score would.

Limitations

While certifications mean that a candidate has a certain set of skills, they probably cannot cover every skill needed for a job. On-the-job, problem-solving skills may be more valuable than a test score.

"Even with a certification, I don't know that people are actually going to have all of the skills [necessary]," says Losco.

According to Johnson, there are IT problems in which "nothing you learn in any book could help you. And I suspect that nothing you learn in any course could help you either. And you're either going to have to involve yourself in a fairly intense tree of logic to try to figure out which factors, when combined, cause the problem. You're going to have to have good contacts with technical support, and basically have a sleuth's mind to figure out what the problem actually is."

Resumes and Cover Letters

CHAPTER 4

The IT Resume

Once you have a degree or certification, and some real-world experience, you'll be ready to apply for your first serious IT job. Usually, whether you even get an interview depends on your resume. You might be the perfect candidate, but not get the job because of a poor resume, or you might be a sub-par candidate and still get the job because of an exceptional resume. We offer two pieces of advice: first, take your resume seriously, don't just throw together a bulleted list; second, keep it succinct, as no one other than the Pope or the President should have more than one page. Remember, the purpose of a resume is just to get you an interview; the interview itself is how you get a job. So don't try to put your life story in the resume.

If you are new to the IT field, your list of qualifications may seem too short. As long as you're applying for an entry-level job, this won't be a problem. Employers will understand that you're new to the field, and they'll be looking for evidence that you can learn the job if hired. Therefore it's still a good idea to include non-relevant work experience, your grade-point average, and a statement of what you hope to get out of the job. All three factors will tell an employer if you will fit in and if you have the raw skills to become the employee they need. In the cover letter, don't just talk about what you can get out of the job, talk about what the employer will get from you!

It's also a good idea to brag a little about any academic research projects you've been involved in, such as testing an old computer science theory with a new application, or a group paper you worked on about microprocessor scalability. Also emphasize any IT projects you've done on the side, such as repairing computers for local small businesses. Similarly, tell potential employers about your extracurricular technology-related interests. Do you build robots, make web sites, or fix your own car? Are you a voracious reader or a successful athlete? Any of these areas are indications of your dedication and leadership skills. But remember that the stronger your technology experience, the less other aspects matter. So if you have some solid college experience, such as internships and help-desk jobs, then it's probably not relevant that you also worked at a pizzeria or played rugby. On the other hand, if you were the treasurer of the university's student government, that might impress a hirer, even though it's not directly related to computers.

Visit Vault at **www.vault.com** for insider company profiles, expert advice, career message boards, expert resume reviews, the Vault Job Board and more.

VAULT CAREER LIBRARY   59

You'll also want to include references and samples of your work. Your references will probably be from professors and any bosses you've had so far. Don't include high school teachers or family friends – that's just unprofessional. Do include samples or summaries of any schoolwork that you're proud of, like a senior or graduate thesis, a software program you wrote or led the direction of, or an electronics part that you designed.

If you're daring, and the company you're applying to has younger managers, then consider taking a more creative approach to stand out from other job applicants. For example, create a web page with a video of yourself and samples of your work. On the page, you can also create a multimedia and hyperlinked resume.

Above all else, re-read your resume and cover letter several times before you click the 'send' button in your e-mail program. Have friends and others read it, especially anyone who you think writes well. Being a solid writer isn't an automatic requirement for getting an IT job, especially an entry-level one, but it definitely helps in showing that you have a solid professional presence. Even if communications skills have no bearing on the job at all, people will automatically eliminate any resume that is poorly written. Keep in mind that good writing isn't just about spelling. Avoid clichés, don't be wordy, and try to use active verbs rather than passive tenses whenever possible. You want to engage the reader and impress them with substance.

Sample Resume

Here's an example of a well-organized resume for a junior network manager's job.

John A. Doe

111 First St., Anytown, CA, 99999

phone: (123) 555-1234

www.thehomeofjohndoe.com / john@thehomeofjohndoe.com

OBJECTIVE: A full-time, entry-level position maintaining multi-platform computer networks at a company offering advancement opportunities

EXPERIENCE:

- Summer 2004: Network management intern, Law Firm Inc. – helped run network of 50 users and 10 servers, helped develop security specifications, installed data backup software

- Sept. 2003-May 2004: Senior helpdesk support, Jane Smith University – supervised team of 15 student consultants, prioritized faculty support issues, performed on-site hardware repair for graduate students

- Summer 2003: Desktop repair technician, Small Real Estate Company Inc. – installed computers and telephones for new agents, helped maintain web site, performed general technical support

- Sept. 2002-May 2003: Junior helpdesk support, Jane Smith University – technical telephone support for undergraduates and the university ISP, helped with freshman IT orientation seminars

- Summer 2003: Sales associate, Anytown hardware store – assisted customers with purchases and checkouts, occasional deliveries, organized data collection system for inventory checks

---

Visit Vault at **www.vault.com** for insider company profiles, expert advice,
career message boards, expert resume reviews, the Vault Job Board and more.

VAULT CAREER LIBRARY   61

ACADEMICS:

- May 2004: BS, Computer Science, Jane Smith University, 3.8 GPA; minor in philosophy – specialized in upperclassmen tracks such as network security, peer-to-peer networking, data backup architecture

- Thesis: "Security in peer-to-peer networks" – 40-page research paper on network security in P2P networks such as Napster and the consequences and lessons for large businesses

- Vice president, JSU High Technology Society – helped organize club special events, organized membership drive, represented JSU at state-wide and national conferences

- Winner, JSU Robotics Competition 2004 – built the JohnDoeBot, competed in tasks such as precise radio-control, navigating an obstacle course, battery life, and PC synchronization functions

- June 2000: Graduate, Anytown High School, National Honor Society member – general college prep curriculum, took electives in Calculus, Physics, World History, and Computer Programming

PERSONAL:

- Wrote my first BASIC program at age 10

- Volunteer network administrator, AnytownNet Wireless

- Hobbies: amateur robotics, lacrosse, piano

Sample E-mailed Cover Letter

Date: Sept. 15, 2004

Subject: Application for junior network manager

From: john@thehomeofjohndoe.com

To: jim_grant@hr.AnytownHospital.com

Mr. Grant,

I'm writing to apply for the junior network manager position advertised today at TechjobseekersRUS.com.

I would be a good fit at Anytown Hospital. I earned a bachelor's degree in computer science this spring from Jane Smith University with a 3.8 grade point average and a minor in philosophy. I specialized in large-scale network design and held several networking and help-desk positions at JSU and in summer jobs.

I'm also knowledgeable about data security, which is very important for patient records. Medical technology and bioinformatics also interest me, and if hired, I'm hopeful that working at a hospital would allow me to learn more about these topics.

Software I wrote and collegiate IT projects I worked on are at my web site, www.thehomeofjohnddoe.com. A resume is attached to this e-mail.

References and other work samples are available.

Thank you,

John Doe

Visit Vault at **www.vault.com** for insider company profiles, expert advice, career message boards, expert resume reviews, the Vault Job Board and more.

V\ULT CAREER LIBRARY   **63**

The IT Interview

CHAPTER 5

Technology interviews are no walk in the park. While there's much variation between interview processes, just as there is between technology employers, many tech interviews contain standard elements – prescreening, tests, brainteasers and peer interviews.

Prescreening

Many HR departments are understaffed and overworked. Before any actual face-to-face interview, many employers use third-party companies to prescreen applicants over the phone.

The prescreening interviewer's job is to filter out candidates, so HR's job becomes more manageable. Many of this interviewer's questions will fish for reasons to keep people out. A question like, "Where do you live?" determines if you would have a long commute that could keep you from getting to the office on time.

Meanwhile, the interviewee must work to win a face-to-face interview. No answers should imply any problems with work, punctuality, personality conflicts, etc.

When asked, "Why did you leave such-and-such past job(s)?" the answer should be truthful but succinct and positive. Concentrate on future opportunities with something like, "I've had great bosses, although not all of them have been easy. But they all learned to rely on me. I'm hoping for another employer like that." If the interviewer asks illegal questions, like ones about family obligations, the interviewee should avoid a confrontation and instead emphasize that such obligations have never been a problem at work.

Without being able to read the interviewer's face or body language, these phone interviews can be challenging. Nevertheless, the interviewee must try to build rapport with the interviewer, because people want to work with people they like. To help themselves out, candidates can and should have their answers ready and in front of themselves when a prescreening interviewer calls.

Tests

Tests are very common for entry-level IT jobs. Sometimes a company will have a standard test for everyone; sometimes the interviewer will test you based on your personal experience and stated ambitions. Sometimes the test will be just a list of multiple-choice questions; other times they'll sit you down in front of a computer and give you a task to complete.

To find the right fit, employers have been using more and more drug tests, background checks, credit checks, and personality tests. According to a survey by Management Recruiters International, 30 percent of companies now use personality tests. There are no right or wrong answers for many of the personality test questions; the employers simply want to see if your personality would fit their offices.

I've seen many different types of tests during IT interviews. Interviewing for an R&D internship in college, someone gave me a coffee mug and told me to make a 3-D drawing of it in AutoCAD. Applying for technical writing work, I've been given editing tests. (I made the mistake of editing a document so heavily that it offended the interviewer – apparently the author was the president of the company.) In another situation, I helped to create a test of open-ended questions for a product reviewer in the telecommunications field. Some people believe it's okay to ask about a test before the interview happens, but I advise against this – if you're qualified for the job, then you shouldn't be worried about taking and doing well on a test.

Peer Interviews

If the prescreening interview goes well, the applicant may face a series of highly technical and intellectually demanding face-to-face interviews. These interviews may make an interviewee wonder where the casual, conversational interviews of the past went. Nowadays, IT companies may send an applicant on several grueling peer interviews in one day.

"[Peer interviews seem] to be very common. It's the whole idea of peer interviewing, that you're interviewed not by a human resources person, but by the people you're going to be working for," says William Poundstone, author of the book, *How Would You Move Mount Fuji? Microsoft's Cult of the Puzzle – How the World's Smartest Company Selects the Most Creative Thinkers.* "There are a lot of good things you can say about [peer interviewing], because really, in a technological field, obviously the people actually in the field are in a better position to assess your experience and skills than someone in human resources."

Peer interviewing does have drawbacks. IT peers are often young and inexperienced at interviewing. "One of the negatives is that you do have these tough interviewers who like flunking people in a way, and I don't think you'd have that if it was human resources people so much," explains Poundstone.

Also, peer interviewers are programmers, database administrators, etc., rather than HR employees who get paid to talk to candidates. "They tend to see this as, you're taking up their time. So, they want to make sure that they make this really hard and they really act as the gatekeeper, making sure that the people that they see as lesser qualified aren't coming into the company," says Poundstone. "At Microsoft and other places, there are people who just like to veto a lot of job applicants by asking really hard questions, and grading them, as it were, on a really tough curve."

Finally, companies can afford to be harsh in interviews. Poundstone warns that some peer interviewers try to shake up candidates, "particularly in companies where they really do know that there's this numerical advantage – that they've got 20 applicants for this one position, and they have this luxury of being very choosy. Some of them just like to rattle applicants. It becomes almost like a fraternity hazing thing, like everyone there has been through this gauntlet of really hard puzzle-type questions, so they're just determined that everyone else after them is going to have to go through this as well."

Peer interviewers want a candidate that fits their environment. Employers are looking for people who complement the manager's personality, and people that fit the team's way of thinking. According to Johnson, "Having 10 people who all think similarly in a group is much easier to manage. And in many ways, it produces higher quality work than if you had 9 people who think the same and one person who's brilliant and who always goes outside of the box, always innovating and always doing new things that the other folks don't understand or don't expect. It becomes, somewhere, that what's best for the group may not be best for the person."

General Interview Questions

All applicants must typically endure questions on salary requirements, where they see themselves in five years, what their biggest flaws are, and how they would describe themselves. The candidates should keep in mind that every answer must relate directly to the job. The jobseekers should study the company and job descriptions a couple days before the interview, to give themselves the extra boost of confidence.

Q: How do you describe yourself?

The answer should concentrate on key, relevant accomplishments that show that the applicant can handle and contribute to the job.

Q: What is your biggest flaw?

This question can be tricky. The answer, "I'm a perfectionist" has been done to death, so employers do not find it useful. "I pay too much attention to detail" is a better answer. Either way, the point of this question is to see how the interviewee deals with problems. Thus, the answer must explain how the jobseeker works to solve things. "I am my own worst critic, but I'm taking time each day to feel good about my accomplishments" is a constructive answer.

Q: Where do you see yourself in five years?

One good answer is "With the same company. I'm looking for a stable, long-term situation."

Q: What are your salary requirements?

There are many possible answers to the salary requirement question. One answer is, "This is my current salary, and I'll consider your best offer." Another possible answer is, "Although I'm at a junior level, I have had good internship and education experiences, and my salary is negotiable." Sometimes, however, employers demand a specific number. In such cases, Internet searches can easily help find salary calculators. Requesting salaries that are too high or too low scare off employers, so median ranges are safest.

Q: Why is your degree in a different field than the work you are pursuing?

The answer could be something like, "That was my academic interest, but my work experience has been in this field." Another possibility is, "I chose a major easily applicable to any field."

Position-Specific Questions

The questions will also vary depending on the position you're applying for. Below, we provide sample interview questions for entry-level positions in desktop support, network support, programming, and work as a webmaster.

Desktop support

Q: What platforms and applications are you experienced with?

Long before you answer this, try to find out the employer's platform preference (what kinds of computers and operating systems they like), and which applications (software) they use. Then answer accordingly. Of course, you don't want to lie. If the company uses some obscure platform that you've never heard of, and software only found in countries that begin with the letter Y, then perhaps it's not the right job for you. More typically, most companies use mainstream platforms like Dell, Hewlett-Packard, IBM, and Sun Microsystems, or they use clones. For operating systems, most companies typically run either a version of Unix, or Windows, or MacOS if they use Apple systems. In software, everyone knows Microsoft Office, but again, try to find out ahead of time what else the company uses, and then learn as much as you can about that software.

Q: What is your approach to PC troubleshooting?

There's not a "right" answer to this question, but in general the most efficient way to do PC troubleshooting is a combination of analytical and empirical methods. Your answer should reflect this, and include some examples of, unique problems you've encountered and how you solved them. You should do some name-dropping of technology terms, so it's clear that you speak the IT staff's language. You should also talk about how you solve problems by collaborating with your peers.

Q: What's your style for dealing with frustrated people?

This question is very important: think about how frustrated YOU feel when technology fails and some smug (or clueless) support agent is trying to help. Smug or clueless are the last things you want to be. So, explain how you'd use patience and politeness to calm the user, how you'd ask questions in a calm but not condescending tone, and how you'd confidently and comprehensively fix the problem. It's OK to use a little humor, as long as you don't seem sarcastic to the person you're trying to help.

Visit Vault at **www.vault.com** for insider company profiles, expert advice, career message boards, expert resume reviews, the Vault Job Board and more.

VAULT CAREER LIBRARY   **69**

You should emphasize that you would ask the user to show you exactly what they were trying to do when the problem happened, and then show them the proper or alternative way of accomplishing the task (don't just emphasize what they did wrong, that insults people's intelligence). When you're finished helping someone, as with any customer support issue, remember that a pleasant demeanor and a smile go a long way toward making people see you as the friendly IT guy, not the obnoxious nerd.

Network support

Q: What kind of networks have you built or maintained?

The most common corporate networks are ones using TCP/IP over Ethernet – that's "transmission control protocol / Internet Protocol" and Ethernet is the physical and data signaling protocol. If you've built a home network (or a wireless network), it probably uses TCP/IP and Ethernet. Start by telling the interviewer about your experience with this. If you've worked with other network types such as Novell, mention that too.

Q: Have you worked with remote access products?

Remote access used to mean just dial-up technologies, but today it also means network access from mobile devices, knowledge of virtual private networks, and knowledge of extranets. Standard dial-up access is becoming obsolete, so just answer honestly if you haven't worked with the newer technologies. However, it would definitely help if you show that you at least know what they are.

Q: What are your thoughts on network security?

Network security is an active and growing field, far beyond the scope of this book. If you don't have any security experience, try to read up on it before the interview.

Junior programmer

Q: Which programming languages do you know?

In academia, most people learn BASIC first, and then advance to more serious languages and tools like C, C++, Cobol, Forth, Java, Pascal, and others. But if you're a self-taught programmer and learned out of the traditional order, many employers value that too. Don't just rattle off a long list of obscure languages – try to list them in some kind logical order, and emphasize the ones that you know best. Also try to emphasize languages that are used in the kind of company you're applying to. For example, if the company does a lot of CADD work, then talk about how you know LISP; if the job involves working with a database, talk about your SQL experience.

Q: Which language is your favorite and why?

This is another question with no right answer. Most programmers have a favorite language, just as an artist has her favorite materials. Talk honestly and passionately about why you prefer Java instead of Microsoft's .Net, or why you enjoy working in C++ more than other languages. It's very important to bolster your preferences with technically sound arguments. It's also okay to talk about how you do understand the merits of a rival language but that you have a simple affinity for the style of another.

Q: What's the most complex program you ever wrote?

Again, just answer honestly. Explain what the program does, why you made it, what language it's written in, and what hardware it runs on. Explain the challenges you faced in designing it, the bugs you encountered, and how you fixed them. Explain how your program (even if it's a game) interacts with other programs. That's important: in the real world, no software acts alone. Most important of all, explain what you learned from writing the program, and explain how you can use that knowledge if hired.

Assistant webmaster

Q: What development languages/tools can you use, other than HTML?

Everyone knows how to make simple web sites in HTML (hypertext markup language) – all you need is Windows Notepad, a copy of HTML for Dummies, and a $10-a-month Yahoo hosting account. It's really very easy, but it's not impressive. Instead, focus on the serious tools that you know how to use, such as Active Server Pages, Flash, JavaScript, and Perl. Show the interviewee that you know how to use these tools for business, not just for fancy graphics and other bandwidth-hogging gunk.

Q: What's your idea of a good web site vs. a lousy one?

Here's your chance to talk about efficient designs and site usability. Talk about your knowledge of how a good web site has powerful back-end tools and infrastructure. Explain how you understand the difference between a web site that just looks like, versus one that actually does something to help people to save money. Talk about site reliability, speed, and software compatibility.

Q: Do you have any creative, design, or editing skills?

Visit Vault at **www.vault.com** for insider company profiles, expert advice, career message boards, expert resume reviews, the Vault Job Board and more.

VAULT CAREER LIBRARY　　**71**

For the customer-facing parts of a web site, it is important to invoke solid creative, design, and editing skills. No matter how good your company's product is, no one will buy them if your web site looks like a bratty child designed it. So bring along screen captures of your own web site, or captures of sites that you think illustrate how to do it right. Also talk about any art or writing experience you have.

When you get a job offer, it's best to say thank you, get all the details, and ask for a day or two to consider it. Unless the job is incredible or you really need to start working immediately, taking time to consider the offer will protect you from taking the wrong job, and might even lead to an offer of more money. When you do begin the job, maintain a low profile until you learn the nuances of the company's (and your boss's) way of doing things.

Brainteasers

Puzzle-style questions enjoy immense popularity in IT interviews. "I get the impression that at least two thirds of [tech] companies tend to ask at least some of these types of questions," says William Poundstone, author of the best-selling book, How Would You Move Mount Fuji? Microsoft's Cult of the Puzzle – How the World's Smartest Company Selects the Most Creative Thinkers. "People have told me that they've had five different interviews, and each [interviewer] asked their favorite three questions. So, you end up doing 15 of these logic puzzles in one day of interviewing."

"There are several reasons [for this popularity]," explains Poundstone. "The one that they usually articulate is that it has something to do with the pace of technological change. There's a feeling that, because the standards are changing so quickly, it's hard to hire someone specifically for one specific skill set. So, they're really looking for mental flexibility, and the ability to deal with new things. And that's what they're hoping to gauge with these types of puzzles."

Also, inexperienced peer IT interviewers tend to look online for trends in interviewing. Microsoft began asking these logic questions of applicants, and others picked up the habit. "I suppose the Microsoft effect has been instrumental in popularizing these types of interviews, just in that there have been all these articles about Microsoft interviewing. And I think that has interested a lot of other companies in this," clarifies Poundstone.

"A third thing is just the whole economic picture, with so many companies downsizing. A lot of companies are finding that they're almost in the position that Microsoft has historically been in: of having very few open positions but an awful lot of applicants. And they're kind of desperate almost to get some systematic way of wading through all those applicants, so they figure that they'll give this a try."

Poundstone warns that this style of interviewing is so new that many interviewers do not know how to handle it. "A lot of companies that don't have a long history of asking these questions will just use that as license to ask any sort of crazy question."

Peer interviewers may ask incredibly difficult questions that do not relate much to the job. "One person said that he was asked, in an engineering job, to describe November," says Poundstone. "And when he pressed the interviewer for some sort of guidance as to what they were looking for, the interviewer just repeated, 'Describe November.' So the guy ended up talking about autumn leaves and Thanksgiving and so forth. Later, the interviewer explained that he had heard somewhere that good engineers give really precise answers. So he wanted something like November is the eleventh month ending twenty-two days before the winter solstice, which seems like a silly interpretation of this question."

However, an interviewer's inexperience may also work in the jobseeker's favor. Interviewers may ask non-effective, one-trick puzzle questions like "the one where you're supposed to take six matchsticks, and arrange them to form four regular triangles," describes Poundstone. "And the intended answer, which is really cute as a puzzle, is that you make a little tetrahedron, or pyramid, so it's three-dimensional. But once you've seen that answer, it's very easy to remember. Particularly in the age of the Internet, you have to figure that people are going to try to Google the answers if they hear about the [puzzle]."

"A lot of people look at these puzzle-type questions as math questions. But it's important to realize that you're going to be graded on them almost as an essay question. They're really looking at your verbal explanation of your approach to the problem. And while they don't expect you to just zero in on the most efficient algorithm, they do expect you to give a good, compelling explanation of what you try, what you do next, and how you bounce back from this idea that didn't work out. And I think there is a real analogy there between that, and how people would solve problems that actually arise in business. So,

Visit Vault at **www.vault.com** for insider company profiles, expert advice, career message boards, expert resume reviews, the Vault Job Board and more.

VAULT CAREER LIBRARY

73

you definitely want to be aware that you're being tested on, in a way, your verbal skills in explaining how you would approach this problem."

Poundstone highlights how to handle a difficult puzzle. "You have to realize that the first idea that pops into your head is probably going to be wrong. And yet, at the same time, you're supposed to be verbalizing your thought process. So, it really unnerves a lot of people, the idea that they're going to be talking about something that is wrong. But the way to deal with that is to introduce the obvious answer that pops into your head, with a tone of skepticism."

"You say, 'Well, the obvious approach would be this,' and then sort of analyze that obvious answer and show why it fails. While you're doing that, it's actually an excellent way of getting to understand the real dimensions of the problem. And usually, by the time you come to the end of the explanation of why that answer is wrong, you'll have an idea of where you want to go to next. So it's a good way of filling the dead air, and it does show your thought process."

ON THE JOB

Career Paths and Days in the Life

In this chapter we take a look at the common career paths and typical days in the life of IT professionals.

Software Development

Career path

As in any field, in this entry-level job out of college, you will be paying your dues by doing routine tasks. Your title will be something like Junior Programmer or Programmer I. You may also begin in a field like quality assurance or support.

Title aside, a typical starting responsibility is debugging code. Debugging is the tedious process of combing through code, keystroke-by-keystroke, looking for mistakes. Not all mistakes will cause software to fail - many just become small annoyances, and others may never be noticed. In this job, the role is mostly that of proofreader; it takes experience to reach a metaphorical copy editor's position, someone who can actually suggest improvements. A typical starting salary may range from $40,000 to $60,000, and the programmer reports to a QA director, or to a product manager. Being asked to work night or weekend shifts is not uncommon.

During the first year or two of debugging and other QA work, the job description also calls for learning all the code being viewed and debugged. It's like being a bench player on a baseball team - just sitting and waiting to play won't advance a career, but acutely observing and learning from the starters will.

The next step is a promotion to Programmer II (or just "programmer"). By this point the programmer actually gets to produce original code, although it's still just coloring inside the pre-drawn lines, making code for someone else's program design. Also, the projects in question are probably upgrades or fixes to existing products, rather than all-new products. But young programmers can begin to build personal libraries of re-useable code and learn some insider tricks of the trade. This is also a good time to learn new programming

Visit Vault at **www.vault.com** for insider company profiles, expert advice, career message boards, expert resume reviews, the Vault Job Board and more.

V/\ULT CAREER LIBRARY   77

languages, or to become a master at one or two. The typical salary ranges from $60,000 to $80,000.

Programmers are assigned to more important projects, and move from being part of a team to leading a team, eventually earning a title like Programmer III or Senior Programmer. Duties include teaching junior programmers, as well as learning to work more closely with the parts of a program that actually touch the hardware, and interact with other related software. These steps may require learning or brushing up on new aspects of computer engineering – veteran programmers can easily get so focused on their job that they fall behind in other aspects of the industry.

Experienced programmers often become software developers. The job here is to actually architect the new software, to achieve the best combination of functionality, speed, and usability - then take the specifications and go write it. In initial development jobs, developers may work on one part of a whole application, before eventually become the person in charge, dreaming up software from a blank screen. They work with product managers and with R&D engineers, in addition to the programmers, and report to senior vice presidents or executives such as the company's CTO. Salaries can reach well over $100,000. Other programmers decide to become senior managers, overseeing other programmers, or set off to start their own businesses.

A Day in the Life: Programmer

"It depends on who you work for, I guess, but around here I am on the early shift by choice. Most folks are on the late shift, though, so that gives me some quiet time to plan my day," says a veteran programmer.

6:30 a.m.: I usually get in right about 6:30 a.m. and start my day by seeing what I missed between 5:00 and midnight the previous day. This usually involves going through about a dozen or two e-mails about the products I work on and listening to one or two voice mails. These are rarely urgent, since folks have my cell phone number and would call me in an emergency.

7:00 a.m.: By 7, I have a pretty good idea about what's in store for the day, but I double check my calendar to make sure I haven't forgotten a meeting or something."

If one of the e-mails or voice messages was about a customer issue, I'll usually get started on that right away. I'll start by looking at the customer service description of the problem and then check to see if the software testing group already knows about a defect that might cause the issue. If I can match the two, I just have to prove that the bug caused the error and let CS know how to fix it, work around it or when it will be fixed in the software.

If the problem is new, I'll have to try and reproduce it and then figure out what caused it. This is usually very quick if the customer and CS described it well, but it can turn into real detective work involving copies of the customer database, WebEx [online conferencing] sessions and phone calls if they didn't.

Usually though, I can spend the next three hours plowing through some development issues like bug fixes or feature development towards the next release or documentation to support those, such as functional requirements, and product specifications.

10:00 a.m.: The morning is usually meeting time. There are team status meetings on Mondays and various product meetings on most of the rest of the days of the week. These take about an hour each, and are usually very effective at advancing the various projects I'm involved in. After each of these meetings is usually an informal breakout with any number of other developers, during which we hammer out details of what was discussed in the meeting, or what wasn't because it was too much detail. After that is lunch and after lunch we usually continue on development efforts (coding or documentation).

2:00 p.m.: Since all of the late-risers are in by now, the afternoons are usually more collaborative, with more informal discussions and meetings about the projects and assignments.

4:00 p.m.: Afternoons are also usually build time, so a couple of days a week there is usually a scramble to check in the latest code and database changes before the build is kicked off. The Software Testing group will get the results of the build and test it so I can expect fresh bugs in the morning. While the build runs I'll have to e-mail the testers about what was changed and what is new for this build.

5:00 p.m.: The day typically ends here when the night shift enters - unless there's a crisis, and the programmer must stay on until it's resolved.

Support

Career path

Being in charge of a company's IT infrastructure is another common goal among entry-level IT professionals. A typical starting point for IT management is the desktop support job. One technician generally supports a few dozen employees, depending on how advanced the employees are and which technology they use. For example, an engineer will fix his own simple computer problems, but he'll require more advanced networking than the mailroom clerk, who may constantly need support for simple issues. Salesmen and remote workers may need special support for laptops and telecommuting problems, such as signing on to the company network from airports.

The support technician spends all day updating software, replacing broken hardware, plugging in telephones for new employees, showing people how to check their e-mail on business trips, and performing virus scans. Many problems can be fixed with a simple reboot. Entry-level IT staff in this role report to senior staff, such as an MIS director, and may make up to $50,000. The days are long, and support techs must ensure that they are always reachable by cell phone, pager, or text message.

After a few years, technical support can get somewhat boring, as the same problems arise over and over. When it's time for a new challenge, support techies often look for a job working with servers, storage, and networks – the next step up. Working on servers requires learning new operating systems, new ways of doing routine maintenance such as installing hard drives, and even new ways of physically installing cables and wires. Maintaining storage requires learning all about backup software and disaster recovery techniques. Meanwhile, monitoring a network requires learning still another class of software, plus the use of special appliance-like tools for testing purposes. This is a good time to seek advanced certifications.

A few more years into such a role qualifies someone to become an IT manager, which means learning the business side of the industry. Instead of just fixing computers, IT managers help executives with purchasing decisions, manage budgets, hire and fire new staff, and meet with technology vendors. They also manage the webmasters, programmers, database administrators, and outside consults and integrators. IT managers are far more indispensable than technicians are, and receive fair pay, approaching six figures or more, depending on the size of the company.

The next challenge is to become an executive-level IT leader – such as a CIO at a larger organization, with multiple offices and hundreds or thousands of employees. This requires learning about things like wide-area networking and storage area networks. It also requires dealing with much larger budgets, spending time justifying decisions to non-technical officers, and working with very detailed security procedures (especially at public-owned companies and government organizations). CIO salaries are usually in low-to-mid six figures, again depending on the company's size and scope.

A Day in the Life: Manager of Technical Services

As the manager of technical services for a major healthcare facility, no two days are alike for Bob Massengill, at the Wake Forest University Baptist Medical Center. "I am responsible for the management and oversight of the hospital's storage area network, IBM mainframe, hardware and operating systems, UNIX hardware and software operations, the disaster recovery initiative, and the all of the patient care systems," he says.

"While the job technically is a Monday through Friday position, our hospital operates 24/7 and requires consistent IT support. Therefore, when I am not in the office, I am on call to support the IT needs of the hospital," he explains. "A typical day is a combination of staff meetings to discuss project status, strategic planning and budgets along with the day-to-day operations of the hospital's IT systems."

6:30 a.m.: Each morning I report in and immediately log in to check the systems I am responsible for, as well as make sure there are not issues with the batch cycles from the night before.

8:00 a.m.: After I am comfortable that all systems are running as they should, I sit down and read my e-mail. While my days all start out the same, they don't play out the same way.

11:00 a.m.- 5:30 p.m.: By the late morning and early afternoon, my day is filled with many tasks, such as supervising seven systems engineers, attending meetings with staff and executives, and meeting with technology vendors. When I leave the office in the evening, I always make sure my phone is forwarded to my pager so that I can be reached in the event of a service interruption or system failure.

Visit Vault at **www.vault.com** for insider company profiles, expert advice, career message boards, expert resume reviews, the Vault Job Board and more.

VAULT CAREER LIBRARY   **81**

"While my days are full, I am also responsible for managing systems implementations, maintenance and testing, which cannot occur during peak hours for the hospital. As a result, we schedule this activity between Saturday night and early Sunday morning, when things are not in high gear. My favorite aspect of my job is working on implementations and upgrades, because it offers a change of pace from the daily routine. It's an opportunity to see a project through from inception to implementation. This is important to me, because I am always thinking about how the work we do can improve the experience for our customers - hospital staff and ultimately, the patient."

"By being aware of how my work affects the patient, some of the most stressful parts of my job happen when we have a system down. It is so important in this environment to ensure that systems can be accessed at all times. I take pride in running an operation that ensures that our patients have a good experience when dealing with all aspects of the hospital - from their care right through to their billing."

Internet Systems Integrator

Career path

Anyone who likes computer networks, solving problems, and being their own boss might be good at this job. The opportunity is clear: there are scores of companies that need to link together disparate computing systems in geographically distributed locations. But it's a long and uphill road to become expert enough to help them.

The best experience for this job is knowledge of potential clients' problems firsthand, through a combination of network management and software development. It's a good idea to work for a large company as early as possible in your career, because being the master of a small company's network just won't teach a broad enough array of skills. For example, integrators on the network side need to understand many different kinds of network protocols, and they need experience with competing brands of routers. They need to become experts at using third-party network management software. On the development side, they need to constantly stay educated about web standards, know enough programming to adeptly utilize application interfaces, and understand database engineering well enough to tie it all together. On top of all that, the solutions they build must have rock-solid security.

It will take some persistence, but working in the data center of a service provider is also a great way to prepare for a career as an independent integrator, because service providers often epitomize the problems of making technology work together. Again, the long-term goal is to become qualified to solve companies' problems of merging conflicting infrastructures, such as when they acquire another company or switch vendors.

No two people take the same route, but a typical path is to work for a large firm like IBM Global Services or EDS, or to work for a regional or industry-specific firm. Associates at such jobs can easily make six figures, with the catch of very frequent travel and long hours. These jobs, simply put, are hard. You don't just show up at a client's site, make everyone move over, and start connecting everything. Typical situations include months of estimating and bidding on the job, months or years of actually implementing new procedures and processes, and ongoing support and training. These deals are frequently worth millions, sometimes even billions of dollars.

A Day in the Life: Web Programmer/ Integrator

The responsibilities of a director of web development cover a mixture of programming, system management, database administration, security implementation, infrastructure design, and project management. Robert Vahid Hashemian is an Internet and database software engineer living in Connecticut. This is a typical day in his life.

9 a.m.: Start the day by checking the various e-mail alerts generated by a number of automatic programs that run overnight. These might include data on the health of servers, activity logs, error logs, and security alarms, among other things. If any of these appear to signal an unusual condition, a deeper investigation might be warranted. I'll try to reproduce the error, the first step toward actually correcting the problem.

10 a.m.: Check e-mails and notes from various departments of any ad hoc projects. Some may require immediate action such as fixing errors, writing programs to generate summary reports, or making changes to existing programs.

Visit Vault at **www.vault.com** for insider company profiles, expert advice, career message boards, expert resume reviews, the Vault Job Board and more.

VAULT CAREER LIBRARY

83

11 a.m.: I meet with departments requesting new projects or fine-tuning existing ones. After the meeting, the project list might have to be tweaked to bump up some projects on the priority list and to downgrade others.

12 p.m.: I work on some project prototypes for demo purposes, allowing the departments to comment on the prototypes before the real work is done.

1 p.m.: I meet with the web designers to get a progress report on their work as they craft various pages for users to interact with. Sometimes this involves coaching them in web languages such as HTML or CSS.

2 p.m.: I start programming some of the web pages, which could include fitting designer's work into web page framework, database wire-up, error handling, and other various programming requirements before the project is ready for release.

4 p.m.: Continue troubleshooting, fixing issues, answering questions, running queries, and generating reports that have been requested throughout the day or are backlogged.

5 p.m.: Phone call to negotiate service levels and pricing with vendors that provide various web products, data circuits, and news feeds. I scrutinize new and ongoing contracts.

Independent Consultants

There are numerous IT consulting contracts under $100,000 available. Most independent consulting contracts come from non-tech, small to medium sized commerce companies. Contracts of this size are typically too small for consulting firms - but just right for independent consultants.

Consultants on this level get lots of different types of work. If a hiring company does not have enough money to update its computer systems, the company may hire consultants to maintain, repair, or operate the legacy systems. When a medium-sized company has enough capital to expand, they usually hire small consultant companies to create e-commerce web sites, databases, internal networks, or medium-scale content management systems.

Independent consultants should be comfortable working with older operating systems and applications. They should also have experience installing and supporting medium-scale networks, office utility applications, and database-driven web sites. Consultants should have experience in technical writing, since they are expected to give lots of technical documentation to the hiring company.

Independent consultants also help companies as analysts. Many companies are looking for people who can phase out ineffective or inefficient products and systems, many of which are legacies from bad consulting advice.

"A good example of this is in the content management field. There's a huge trend where companies buy a content management product, and it never even gets implemented," explains John Running, CEO of MobiusWEB, an independent consulting company that creates databases, version-control software, and web sites. "Either the product wasn't implemented properly, or whoever sold it didn't focus on meeting the customer's needs."

"I realized that the thing to do is to spend more time interviewing the people who would use the software, and stay inexpensive," explains Running. "I sold a content management system to the American Ballet Theater this way. Big consulting firms charge insane amounts of money to spend time talking to the customers. The hiring companies are much better off talking to a small consultant like you."

Medium sized companies usually pay consultants around $30,000 to $100,000 to create or replace software and system solutions. In a slow economy, companies are likely to scale back on six-figure projects, but they will probably continue to outsource for smaller IT projects. Large consulting firms usually do not bother at all with contracts under $50,000, so independent consulting firms can find lots of business in this market.

"IBM isn't going to go after a $30,000 or $40,000 project. But there are an awful lot of companies out there who need thirty and forty thousand dollar projects done," says Brad Smith, Vice President of Research for *Consulting* magazine. "So, the smaller niche firms who have very little overhead, and can act very nimbly, and cost competitively, are going to succeed in this sort of environment."

However, hiring companies only want to hire consultants with proven track records. Thus, new consultants who do not have portfolios or business references usually have to work for smaller contracts under $10,000. Companies that hire these green consultants are usually new themselves, and do not have the capital to go with more experienced consultants. These customers may be hard to work with, as they still need to get their own bearings together. Consultants here must learn how to deal with customers

Visit Vault at www.vault.com for insider company profiles, expert advice, career message boards, expert resume reviews, the Vault Job Board and more.

VAULT CAREER LIBRARY   85

quickly if they want to make a good impression and gain professional references. Beginner consultants may have to scrape for business in this manner for a year or two before they have enough credentials to catch the attention of larger companies.

Independent Engineering Consultant

As big IT consulting firms struggle with slow growth projections and an unfavorable economy, the experience requirements for joining one of them becomes increasingly demanding. Jobseekers hoping to break into IT may find creating or joining a small, independent IT company a more attractive choice. Or they might decide it's more worthwhile to incorporate themselves and do freelance IT work (more on how to do that in the section on companies below). Smaller IT consulting companies can thrive in the markets below $100,000.

John Running is the founder of MobiusWEB, an IT consulting company that creates and sells content management systems, database architecture, and web sites. MobiusWEB has made the web sites of the American Ballet Theater (www.abt.org), Junior's cheesecake restaurant in New York City (www.juniorscheesecake.com), and *Blender* (www.blender.com), a magazine in the *Maxim* magazine franchise. His company consists of three mainstay people, with Running the chief engineer and programmer. Depending on the day, Running's waking hours can be monopolized by anything from coding to sales.

A non-engineering day

Like many consultants, Running first learned how to engineer and program. Then, he decided to incorporate himself and become an independent consultant. With his new job title came the need to learn many business skills.

"Eighty percent of what I do is not programming," stresses Running. "In my business, I have to be everything; CTO, CEO, salesman, everything. I multi-multitask." Consequentially, most days, John Running is not an engineer.

"When we do a project, we have a workflow," says Running. "I wouldn't start developing a program for a company until they sign off on the design schematics and the information architecture and everything, so we'd know exactly what it is that we are supposed to do."

Thus, Running says he uses non-development days "to go meet up with clients, where I'll spend a lot of time with them. Possibly having multiple meetings per day, going all over the city."

Meetings

Sales meetings will be particularly challenging for newcomers in the field of IT consulting. Customers only want to deal with consultants they know are reliable. Consultants who do not have name recognition must work to impress customers in a very short amount of time or else lose a contract. Even beginner consultants must have a web site and a portfolio of successfully completed projects, even if the projects were done in school.

Most importantly, newcomers should have references ready. "The [American Ballet Theater] checked four of my references very thoroughly," says Running. "I provided them with four, and they checked them all. And all of those people had positive things to say. That was the reason I got that job."

Once a consultant makes a sale, he or she must meet with the client again to plan the project. Surviving such a client meeting takes more than technical know-how. "If I had to point at one thing that has caused me to be in any way successful in this business, it's having some skill at understanding the requirements of my clients, with a scant amount of input," says Running. "With very little input about what their business is, I have to make a system that will somehow accommodate them or will meet their requirements completely."

The rest of the day

In between the meetings, traveling, and pitching, Running is still working. "I've written a lot of documentation, and that breaks up a lot of my day too. Writing up scopes of work, reviewing bills, making sure those are correct."

Having all these duties makes the independent consultant's day much longer than the usual programmer's. "I keep kind of crazy hours. I have to wear many, many hats. It's a lot of responsibility, but I have to do all that. I charge $100 an hour, and generally all my time is filled."

An engineering day

"A typical day, when I'm in my programming phase, is to sleep in late, and start coding as soon as I get up," says Running. "I code in spurts of three to four hours, eat sometimes, and code until two or three in the morning. Trying as best I can to have as little contact with any of my customers as possible."

Visit Vault at www.vault.com for insider company profiles, expert advice, career message boards, expert resume reviews, the Vault Job Board and more.

VAULT CAREER LIBRARY   **87**

Maintaining a small IT consulting firm can result in odd, in addition to long, hours. Running keeps odd hours on purpose. "If I only really start working towards the middle of the day, then that's only a certain number of hours in which clients are around to talk to me," explains Running. "So I'm still around to answer them, so I don't come off like a derelict. But then I have all those hours after they go home to work on stuff, and I'm still rested."

This can be a challenge if the IT consultant does not have help. "That's one of the reasons why I took on my current business partner," says Running. "He was willing to work very hard and take on so many of the roles of dealing with these customers, allowing me the time to program when I have to."

With administrative concerns taken care of by others, engineering days still offer their own hardware and programming challenges. For Junior's, each box shipment could hold six cheesecakes. However, "because of the legacy database system the company used, we could only have as many as five different kinds of cheesecakes in any one box. So we built a database to store all this information," relates Running. "And the different shipping prices didn't fit an algorithm, so we had to create an array that pulled in prices for each one." These are typical problems; IT consulting firms are often hired to deal with legacy or out-of-date systems.

With experience, day-to-day engineering should become simpler. "Once I have a bunch of code written for a bunch of clients, and they all essentially have the same problems and requirements, then it's a whole lot easier to recycle the old code than it is to write new stuff from scratch."

Day after day

For people running small IT consulting companies, these long days are the norm. "I work pretty much every day of the week," says Running. "I've worked over 100 hours a week for as long as I can remember now."

Running warns that this can be rough. "Do I think that many people would want to live the life that I've been living? No! I don't think it's very suited to most people," clarifies Running. "I'm willing to work for a very long time, because I believe that what I want is hard to attain. But I'm also pompous and crazy enough to believe that I can get it."

But Running says that he is willing to endure these days for non-economic reasons too. "I enjoy writing ASP, I enjoy writing database models, I enjoy spending time with editors of magazines. And if people look at the web site, and it's useful, and it doesn't crash, and the customers are happy, then it's a big success," explains Running. "That's the kind of thrill that I feel like most people never even have. It's the kind of thrill you get from having tried very hard, spending a lot of energy, and empathizing, and caring, and having all of that really work out in a very meaningful way."

John Running tells Vault about his learning experience planning the web site for Junior's Restaurant in Brooklyn, a restaurant famous for its cheesecakes.

"Selling cheesecakes over the Internet - I'm sure that sounds like a very simple kind of IT problem. Right? But, for a number of reasons, it wasn't. Most people wanted to buy cheesecakes as gifts, to buy multiple items, and to send them to many different people. And they also wanted to specify - if they were giving them as gifts - when the cheesecakes would arrive. They didn't want to just buy them and have them shipped out that day necessarily. And because shipping is generally based on weight, it's not really feasible to just associate one, fixed shipping price with any given product. We had to set up a system that accounted for them being able to fit six different cheesecakes in one package.

Such client meetings can be a perilous place for the inexperienced. "Unless you are diligent, or are in a position to know when there's a real gap in the understanding, you're at the terrible risk of creating something for them that doesn't meet their requirements at all," says Running. "And what happens is that either the contract changes, or you, as the unlucky developer, have to do way more work than you ever anticipated doing, and are at risk of going out of business."

IT Manager

OK, so you've reached the midpoint of your technology career and you're no longer relegated to doing routine tasks – you now tell people what to do. What's your job like?

On the surface, an IT manager's day may seem to be no different than any corporate manager's. Looking deeper, however, a day in IT management offers one unique challenge after another. After all, the IT manager makes sure that the myriad of people in technology, the corporate departments, and the company think tanks work smoothly together.

Visit Vault at **www.vault.com** for insider company profiles, expert advice,
career message boards, expert resume reviews, the Vault Job Board and more.

V∧ULT CAREER LIBRARY   89

Ingrid Johanns is the IT manager who standardizes all of Chevron-Texaco's web sites. Her main duties are the same as those all IT managers must perform: standardizing technology, managing teams of techies, and being the voice between technology and business. Her day is typical of an effective manager's.

"I don't think my day is very interesting," says Johanns modestly. "It's like, write e-mail, check e-mail, get on the phone, call people, walk around, walk to a meeting, have a meeting." But each of those events is actually surrounded by decisions, dilemmas, and the need for ingenuity that characterizes an expanding technology field.

Johanns' task to standardize Chevron-Texaco's entire web site is as typical and as demanding as it gets for managers. Chevron-Texaco is a worldwide, non-IT company that recently merged. Its IT departments are spread across the globe.

"Part of it is, I have to find where all the web people are in the company," says Johanns. "It's almost the same thing as saying, 'I'm going to standardize the In-TER-net! Where would I start? Well, I'll start at Yahoo.com, and I'll follow all the links! Hopefully, all the web site owners put their contact information on their sites.' That's the kind of challenge that it is."

That challenge is by no means unique, considering that nine out of ten IT jobs are at non-IT companies. And, since the market is slow for IT consulting of that magnitude, it is often up to managers like Johanns to handle projects like this.

After finding the proper managers and programmers to call, "the next thing is approaching them, and approaching them in the right way," says Johanns. "But not in a too demanding, 'you! You have been spotted on our radar! You must change your web site immediately or we will pull the plug!'"

Finding the right approach may be tricky. "People hate change. And there are things that aren't very nice about [site-wide] standards; it takes away your freedom."

Thus, Johanns must put the technology people at ease about having to change their web site procedures and methods. Unfortunately, it can be tough defusing resistance to new standards and policies.

"I've gone into meetings where, in the very beginning, arms are crossed," says Johanns. "They're looking at me all nasty, and they're like, 'my boss told me I had to come to this! I'm going to sit here and listen to it, but I'm not going to do anything. I'm not going to change that web site ever! You're just taking away my freedom and this makes absolutely no sense! This is a big waste of time for the company!'

Finding the right approach means doing more work before the initial meeting. "I go and I gather information from all these people," says Johanns. "I have them fill out a questionnaire, where I say, 'So, what do you like about standards? What don't you like? What are your opinions on this?' I basically poll them, and try to get a psychographics demographic on where they stand in regards to the standards."

So then, the opposition remains against specifics in the policies, but not to the IT manager implementing them. "My approach has been to really embrace all the resistance. Instead of resisting the resistance, I go right up to them, and say, 'Thank you! Thank you for the resistance!'"

"But not everybody's going to speak up necessarily," says Johanns. "They might be afraid I'm going to hold it against them. They might be afraid I'll tell their boss, or that I'd say, 'Look! You said you didn't like them! You're fired!'" So Johanns must work hard to strike the right tone during meetings.

"Walk to a meeting, have a meeting"

Once the proper people have been found, approached, polled, and notified of the project, the next step is to lay out the project details in a meeting. "When we get into the session, it's like a three-hour training session about the new standards," says Johanns.

"What I do, in the very beginning, is I get them into little groups," says Johanns. "And I have them all talk about what they think of the standards. Basically, I just get them talking with each other – and with me not there, either."

Johanns uses this method to get the meeting participants to speak freely about their opinions. "And they're getting their issues out," explains Johanns. "One goal is to just have them voice their issue, and then also to hear what their peers think."

After discussion begins, Johanns begins to visit each small group. "And I talk about their issues. I ask, 'What don't you like about them?'"

Once again, Johanns embraces the resistance. "It does suck if you're a designer and you're used to doing whatever you want," says Johanns. "So I acknowledge their concern, I don't just ignore it. And then I say, 'We're going to talk about that actually.' And then I go through the presentation."

Visit Vault at www.vault.com for insider company profiles, expert advice, career message boards, expert resume reviews, the Vault Job Board and more.

VAULT CAREER LIBRARY   91

Johanns claims that acknowledgement is key. "The philosophy of being really open to criticism to the standards, and being open to people not liking it, it makes the [participants] really open to me."

"I've gone into groups where they're really upset with me at first," describes Johanns. "And then, by the end of the session, they're like, 'Let me show you what I'm working on! What do you think of this?' They're asking my advice! They're my friends."

"Walk around"

After holding a meeting, Johanns must do more legwork. Not all questions can be answered in a meeting.

"People ask things like, why do we need to use these colors?" says Johanns. "It makes sense that you'd limit the palette, but why was it limited like that? Why that blue, and that red?"

To get the answers, Johanns goes to other offices, like the branding department. There, she asks the same questions that were posed to her. "I'm like, where do these colors come from? Why should we use them? You give me the arguments because I don't know. I have no good response to people who say they don't want to use them."

In an effort to deal with the technology people, Johanns learns more about the corporate side of the company. "I got all this information on how corporations pick colors and how they have to look at what competitors' colors are," says Johanns. "They did do a great job of coming up with what the standards should be. So it's been easy for me to go and look up the reasons for why something is a certain way."

"But, the thing is, just having a high quality product, and having a good business case behind it, does not guarantee that it's going to be successful," stresses Johanns. "It's all in the way it's presented and dealt to people."

"Write e-mail, check e-mail"

After getting people on board with the project, and after getting them started on the work, IT managers still have a lot to do in the day. To ensure that IT departments finish their jobs on time, IT managers must continually follow up with their technology people.

"I'm like a helpdesk for standards, making myself available to the technology people so that we can keep in touch," says Johanns. "Because even if the seminar went really great, a couple days later the [technology workers] may get distracted and may not follow through on what they're doing. Or they might get back into their old way of thinking."

As a support person for the company's web standards, Johanns also keeps an eye on the technology. "The other piece is evolving the standards. When I discover things that aren't working, or things that need to be tweaked, or changed, then I need to manage that process as well."

Once the technology people are working on the project, and become used to touching base with the manager, the manager's job becomes easier. "I feel like I'm at the point where I've gotten momentum on the project, a lot of web sites are being redone, and I don't see nearly the amount of resistance I did in the beginning," says Johanns. "In fact, sometimes my presentation at times seems almost heavy-handed in trying to convince them. Because they're all already here going, 'Yeah, this is a good thing, we're okay.'"

Lifestyle in Tech

CHAPTER 7

Working in technology, you'll quickly find that some aspects of the lifestyle are very different from what you expected, and that others are exactly what you expected – maybe even stereotypical. For example, working as a support technician at rural city hall, at a medium-sized law firm, and at a global engineering services corporation will be very different experiences, even though your title and job description are the same. The same is true for social aspects, dress code, stress level, and career path.

Irregular schedules

Many jobs in IT require you to work non-standard hours. For example, if you work for a large or international company that develops technology, they'll likely have shifts, as in developers who work from 7 a.m. to 4 p.m., programmers who work from 4 p.m. to 11 p.m., and then overseas testers who work the next eight hours. That way, the developers come to work the next morning, and the things they designed and planned for are programmed, tested, and ready for the next cycle. If you work in IT for a company that just uses technology, you'll be expected to be always available, whether by cell phone, pager, or e-mail (which are all integrated into single products these days anyway). Even in non-emergency situations, you'll still have to work some weekends or nights, which is when IT staff tend to test new products or perform major system upgrades. (That way, it doesn't interfere with the regular course of business.)

Stress

Working in IT can be a crash course in diplomacy and precious "people skills." Many of your colleagues will approach technological challenges differently. For some people, the bottom line is to get technology to work, no matter how ugly the solution (known as a kluge). Other people won't rest until they've solved an IT problem elegantly. Still others won't rest unless the solution is efficient and provides cost savings.

Dealing with stress is a big part of any IT job, whether your role is junior desktop support or CTO. The so-called IT "fires" occur constantly. People run to you, call you, e-mail you, page or text-message you, interrupt your family vacation to Disney World.

Visit Vault at **www.vault.com** for insider company profiles, expert advice, career message boards, expert resume reviews, the Vault Job Board and more.

VAULT CAREER LIBRARY   95

Injury

Aside from merely annoying daily tension, IT stress can result in physical injury. This is a serious issue that made "ergonomics" a household word. Spending too much intense time using a computer can cause injury to your back, eyesight, fingers, and neck (along with your heart and waistline, given that stressful IT positions often result in quick and unhealthy snacking in lieu of real lunches.) The U.S. Department of Labor's Occupational Safety and Health Administration offers advice and resources at www.osha.gov/SLTC/computerworkstation/otherresources.html, as does the Mayo Clinic at www.mayoclinic.com.

Sites like www.healthycomputing.com also provide useful information. Using even more technology can help too, as there are many products on the market designed to help you sit, type, and view in healthier and more ergonomic ways. There's even an International Ergonomics Association (www.iea.cc) and trade conventions (www.ergoexpo.com). Ergonomics and human safety also features in the study of "Human-Computer Interaction," better known as HCI. HCI also has its share of companies and conferences. A good place to learn more is at www.hcibib.org.

IT culture and stereotypes

Technology is more of a meritocracy than most other industries. And while spirited debates on technology subjects (known in the industry as "holy wars") inevitably occur, most employers discourage this kind of contention, especially at large companies in which large and disparate computing systems must literally work together. So try to keep this in mind when you show up for your new IT job.

Unfortunately, IT suffers from more gender stereotyping than many other industries. Though women are successfully employed at all levels of the IT industry and have been for many years, and though there are also many significant industry leaders who are female, pockets of political incorrectness persist among men in the field. Examples range from men who wouldn't intentionally offend people, but who simply lack good social skills, to men who feel that only they can do solid IT work. That's not to say that the IT industry tolerates inappropriate behavior any more than other fields, but it's hard to deny that as long as there are introverted male computer nerds, there will be inappropriate beliefs about women. The good news is that this is changing, largely due to the influx of women during the Internet boom and the attrition (by age and layoffs) of the he-man women haters club.

Off-hours labor, and the sporadic eating habits this precipitates, are factors more specific to IT. There is a stereotype of the single male IT worker surrounded by empty bottles of Coke and half-eaten Twinkies. There are many cases where this is absolutely true. But there are just as many cases where it's completely false. Yes, there are scores of real nerds, but there are also health nuts, family men, women, and fitness enthusiasts.

Moving up

After you've paid your dues with a few years of entry-level IT work, you'll naturally desire to move up the career ladder. So what do you do about it? You might become a niche specialist, move up into management, take a similar job at a bigger company, or even start your own company. In general, having experience and certifications and cultivating good relationships with coworkers, managers and clients will always work in your favor.

Becoming a specialist can be lucrative if you choose the right area. If you became a data storage expert in the mid-1990s, then you'd be very successful today, as that segment skyrocketed in demand while the supply of experts was low. But if you became an expert in IBM's OS/2 operating system, you'd be in big trouble today, as that platform is virtually extinct. There are similar choices to make today: should you specialize in programming for the Palm or Microsoft handheld devices? Are peer-to-peer networks just a fad, or a lasting corporate technology? Will desktop computers from Apple and mainframes from IBM become extinct in 10 years, or will they thrive?

Becoming a manager is an equally popular route for IT staffers. Basically you'll move from being a generalist in IT to being the boss of a few generalists.

Another way to rise up in the IT industry is to start your own company. There are all kinds of success stories, from the "traitorous eight" who formed Fairchild Semiconductor after a falling out with William Shockley, co-inventor of the transistor, to Steve Jobs and Steve Wozniak, the latter of whom left Hewlett-Packard to found Apple Computer when (as the story goes) HP assured him they had no interest in personal computers. It's easy to find examples of success, but it's exponentially easier to identify technology startups that fell down before they could walk. However, there are thousands of companies in the middle, founded by mid-career IT workers who simply make a living, but who don't strive to become huge corporations. If you examine a Yahoo directory or a traditional phone book, for every big company's display advertisement, there are hundreds of one-line, simple

Visit Vault at **www.vault.com** for insider company profiles, expert advice, career message boards, expert resume reviews, the Vault Job Board and more.

VAULT CAREER LIBRARY   **97**

entries. The moral is, if you have an idea for a feature that your IT employer says isn't worthwhile, or if you want to explore an IT specialty that's not needed at your current job, then you should strongly consider doing it on your own, or helping others do it by becoming an independent consultant.

APPENDIX

Organizations

Listed below are some of the biggest IT industry groups. There are also many specialty groups for specific applications, industries, and regions, but those are too numerous to list here. Marketing groups disguised as user or technical groups are yet another category, as are the international standards-setting bodies.

- Association for Computing Machinery (ACM) – www.acm.org

- Association of Shareware Professionals – www.asp-shareware.org

- Association for Women in Computing – www.awc-hq.org

- Computer & Communications Industry Association – www.ccianet.org

- Computing Technology Industry Association (CompTIA) – www.comptia.org

- Information Technology Association of America – www.itaa.org

- Institute of Electrical and Electronics Engineers (IEEE) – www.ieee.org

- Usenix Association (Unix user group) – www.usenix.org

Recommended Resources

Do-it-yourself

- DriverGuide.com
- EnGadget.com
- Gizmodo.com
- Nuts & Volts (magazine)
- PC Mag (magazine)
- PC World (magazine)
- Tomshardware.com
- The-gadgeteer.com
- Tucows.com

News and trends

- CNET (www.cnet.com and www.news.com)
- Computerworld (magazine)
- eWeek (magazine)
- Information Week (magazine)
- Network World (magazine)
- The New York Times (Thursday "Circuits" section)
- SiliconValley.com
- Slashdot.org (news about open-source)
- Wired (magazine)

History

- *Collectible Microcomputers*, by Michael Nadeau (Schiffer, 2002)

- *Dealers of Lightning: Xerox PARC and the Dawn of the Computer Age*, by Michael Hiltzik (HarperCollins, 1999)

- *ENIAC: The Triumphs and Tragedies of the World's First Computer*, by Scott McCartney (Walker, 1999)

- *Fire in the Valley: The Making of the Personal Computer*, by Paul Frieberger and Michael Swaine, (McGraw-Hill, 1999)

- *Hackers: Heroes of the Computer Revolution*, by Steven Levy (Penguin Putnam, 2001)

- *The Chip: How Two Americans Invented the Microchip and Launched a Revolution*, by T.R. Reid (Random House, 2001)

- *Turing and the Universal Machine: The Making of the Modern Computer*, by Jon Agar (Icon, 2001)

- *When Information Came of Age: Technologies of Knowledge in the Age of Reason and Revolution, 1700-1850*, by Daniel Headrick (Oxford, 2002)

- *The New Hacker's Dictionary*, by Eric S. Raymond (MIT Press, 1996)

Tech Glossary

Throughout this book there are many terms that may be unfamiliar, but which you should learn. For more tech vocab, check out Webopedia.com.

32/64-bit: Term referring to the data size of a microprocessor's address bus (an address bus is the part that translates computer programming into actual raw data).

Alpha: The first primary test version of a computing system.

API: "Application programming interfaces" are programs to help other people connect to your own program.

Appliance: Any networked computing system that ships on custom hardware.

Autonomic: A term favored by IBM, meaning computing systems that fix themselves.

Backup: The technique of making copies of data at regular intervals, for safety.

Beta: The second, almost-finished version of a computing system.

Binary: The most common numerical system (using only 0 and 1) in computers.

Black lists: Software for blocking specific e-mail addresses.

Certification: An official statement of your expertise from a standards body.

Chargeback: A technique for tracking how much of a computing system a department is using, based on corporate budgets.

Cluster: A group of identical computing systems, linked together for reliability.

Coding: A slang term for programming.

Compiler: Special software for translating programs into raw data.

CRM: "Customer relationship management" is the trend of using technology to give customers better support while also saving money for your company.

CTI: "Computer-telephony integration" is the trend of merging computer technologies with telecommunications for a wide range of new products and services.

Data warehousing: The hardware/software equivalent of a big room full of databases.

Database: The software equivalent of a filing cabinet.

DBA: A "database administrator."

Developer: A person who designs the concept and planning of computing systems, which are then built by programmers (similar to the rlationship between an an architect and a builder).

Digital: Any calculation represented by numbers instead of by direct variables (keeping in mind that computing systems are just advanced calculators at heart).

.Net: Pronounced as "dot net" -- Microsoft's proprietary version of Web services.

Encryption: The technique of making data unreadable to anyone who doesn't have a special "key."

Fibre channel: A high-speed networking technology, mostly used for a SAN.

Firewall: Hardware/software combinations to protect a network from outside attacks.

Gigabit Ethernet: A high-speed networking technology (also, 10 gigabit ethernet, which is exponentially faster and more expensive).

Hacker: A person who enjoys working on machines for the pure education and thrill of it (largely distorted by the media to mean "a high-tech criminal").

Hands-on imperative: The concept that you can only learn by trying something for yourself.

Holy wars: Any debate of "which is better" among technology workers.

Interconnects: High-speed technology for passing data directly between computers' memory, also known as remote direct memory addressing (RDMA).

Legacy: Any computing system that's considered old or just isn't used anymore.

Licensing: The process of purchasing permission from a technology company to use a certain amount of their product for a certain length of time.

Linux: A freely distributed, Unix-like operating system, where anyone can make changes but they must share those changes with everyone.

Load balancing: The technique of sharing the computing workload across computing systems.

NAS: Servers specially designed for storing data, often built as appliances.

Open-source: The concept of sharing programs freely with anyone, as long as people also share any changes or improvements they make in the program.

Operating system: Oversimplified, it means the primary software that people use to interface with a computer, on top of which other software resides.

Outsourcing: The concept of paying a specialty company to administer your company's IT.

PBX: A "personal branch exchange" means a business phone system.

"Putting out fires": The industry phrase for dealing with the various IT emergencies that happen throughout a typical day.

Program: A list of computer code that makes the machine do something (also known as software or applications).

Programming: The craft of creating computer software by mastering a language.

Routers: Technology for passing data between network segments.

SAN: "Storage area networks" are sets of special-purpose computers for storing data accessible via networks.

Server: A business-class computer that holds data or programs for other computers to use.

Solaris: A popular version of Unix, owned by Sun Microsystems.

SQL: "Structured query language" is a popular way to interact with a database.

SSL: "Secure sockets layer" is another network security standard; when used with a VPN, it eliminates the need for the user to have any special programs.

Tape library: Computing systems using very large magnetic tape technologies for storing important, but rarely used (or just old) data.

"The build": Slang term for the most recent version of a compiled program.

Unified messaging: The combination of e-mail, voice-mail, and faxing into one product.

Unix: A text-based operating system known for its reliability (compared to Windows); Unix has many variations or "flavors."

Virtualization: A technique for managing many physical computing systems as one virtual system; also, a technique for managing one physical computing system as many virtual systems.

VoIP: Telecommunications conducted over computer networks instead of traditional phone lines, to save money.

VPN: A way to create a secure connection over a non-secure (public) network.

Web services: An evolving set of tools used for programming Internet-centric computing systems.

White lists: Software for allowing specific e-mail addresses.

Windows: The family of graphical operating systems from Microsoft.

XML: "Extensible markup language" is a translator technology for any networked computing system, but mostly for web sites.

About the Authors

Tod Emko

For nearly a decade, Tod Emko has developed database, software, and hardware solutions for a variety of companies. He has written columns in several national publications, including the *XML-Journal,* and currently writes for technical sites and magazines, while also programming for Toasted Pixel Inc., a New York City web site development company. Emko holds a bachelor's degree in linguistics and a minor in computer science from New York University, and he holds a master's degree in journalism from Syracuse University.

Evan Koblentz

Evan Koblentz is a freelance technology writer in the New York City area, and edits the Computer Collector Newsletter. He's been a reporter for Ziff-Davis and Gannett, and was technology editor and a staff engineer at TMC Labs. Evan has a BA in English and a minor in technology from Kean University, and attended graduate school for journalism at Boston University. He's fond of fast cars, dark beer, and bad science fiction.

Losing sleep over your job search? Endlessly revising your resume? Facing a work-related dilemma?

Use the Internet's
MOST TARGETED
job search tools.

Vault Job Board

Target your search by industry, function, and experience level, and find the job openings that you want.

VaultMatch Resume Database

Vault takes match-making to the next level: post your resume and customize your search by industry, function, experience and more. We'll match job listings with your interests and criteria and e-mail them directly to your inbox.

VΛULT
> the most trusted name in career information™

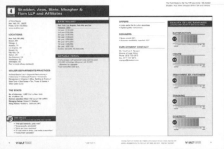